P9-BYO-734

ALSO BY WANDA AND GIOVANNA TORNABENE

La Cucina Siciliana di Gangivecchio (with Michele Evans)

Sicilian Home Cooking (with Michele Evans)

ALSO COAUTHORED BY CAROLYNN CARREÑO

Once Upon a Tart (with Frank Mentesana and Jerome Audureau)

100 Ways to Be Pasta

SE 28 '05

641.822
TOR

100 Ways to Be Pasta

PERFECT PASTA RECIPES FROM GANGIVECCHIO

Wanda and Giovanna Tornabene

WITH CAROLYNN CARREÑO

BARRINGTON AREA LIBRARY
505 N. NORTHWEST HWY.
BARRINGTON, ILLINOIS 60010

 ALFRED A. KNOPF • NEW YORK • 2005

THIS IS A BORZOI BOOK
PUBLISHED BY ALFRED A. KNOPF

Copyright © 2005 by Wanda Tornabene and Giovanna Tornabene

Photographs copyright © 2005 by Carolynn Carreño

All rights reserved under International and Pan-American Copyright Conventions. Published in the United States by Alfred A. Knopf, a division of Random House, Inc., New York, and simultaneously in Canada by Random House of Canada Limited, Toronto. Distributed by Random House, Inc., New York.

www.aaknopf.com

Knopf, Borzoi Books, and the colophon are registered trademarks of Random House, Inc.

Library of Congress Cataloging-in-Publication Data

Tornabene, Wanda.

100 ways to be pasta : perfect pasta recipes from Gangivecchio / Wanda and Giovanna Tornabene with Carolynn Carreño.

p. cm.

Includes index.

ISBN 1-4000-4104-X

1. Cookery (Pasta)   2. Cookery, Italian—Sicilian style.   I. Tornabene, Giovanna.   II. Title.

TX809.M17T6 2005

641.8'22—dc22   2004048522

Manufactured in Singapore

First Edition

To all those Italians who have moved to America with their lives and memories in boxes and baggage tied up with string. We like to think that a dish of spaghetti, shared around a table, will turn your thoughts to the tender caress of your faraway country.

For us Italians, pasta is a live thing. It is not something we eat by choice, but by default, like spending time with an old friend or a beloved family member. Pasta is not just a food, it is a comfort. There is nothing else like it. If you have troubles, you sit down to a bowl of pasta, and the minute you begin to twirl the spaghetti on your fork, you begin to untie your problems.

CONTENTS

OPPOSITE: *This stone fountain, built in 1778, lies just outside the abbey gates and provides us with sweet natural spring water year-round.*

ACKNOWLEDGMENTS

A simple thank-you to all those people who collaborated on this book by improving our lives in some way. Since for us it is sometimes difficult to separate life from food, this is a tribute to those who have made both of those things so much better.

Thanks to Michele Evans Plesser and to her husband, Tully. Although Michele is not with us in this third book, she is always in our hearts as a perfect example of friendship, love, and generosity. We know we can always count on them.

Thanks to Peter Gethers, our editor, and to Janis Donnaud, our agent. Without them, this book simply would not exist. And even if life sometimes plays its tricks on human beings, these things will never cut the deep feeling between us.

Thanks to Carolina Carreño, our new coauthor. We shared with her a piece of our life in Gangivecchio, and she shared with us her talent and patience.

Thanks to all the people at Knopf for the passion they put into their work and the exceptional product that comes of this.

Thanks to all the friends and relatives on this island where we live and work, and where forever we will have the warmth of their assistance and their presence.

Thanks to the crew who live and work with us. This includes our little animals, the dogs and cats that bring joy to our souls every day.

And last, thanks to Gangivecchio, an endless source of ideas and of love.

It was on a summer afternoon over dinner at Gangivecchio that our agent, Janis Donnaud, suggested we write a third book—this one about pasta. "There's nothing more Italian than pasta," she said. And this is true. Pasta is so basic for us that Mamma and I wondered if we had anything to tell people about pasta that they didn't already know. Janis and her partner, our editor Peter Gethers, assured us that based on what they had seen and tasted during the hundreds of meals we have prepared for them, we did. When they told us this, we became very enthusiastic.

We imagined that to write a book about pasta would be as natural as breathing. We know so much about this food, the most famous product of our country. We know its history and everything there is to know about cooking pasta. Inventing new ways to prepare pasta with an innate sense of what will work and what will not—this seems to be part of our genetic code as Sicilians and as Italians.

We know pasta so well that it is in our heads the way that every educated person carries simple mathematic formulas and uses them every day without knowing it. One liter of water for one hundred grams of pasta, five to ten grams of salt for every liter of water. Eighty grams of pasta for every person. We walk to the pasta drawers that are filled with so many different shapes of pasta, we choose the shape we want, weigh it on the antique scale that is central to our kitchen (and our cooking), salt the water, stir the pasta to prevent it from sticking together. We taste from time to time as it cooks because thirty seconds underdone and the pasta is tough and chewy. Boiled too long and it becomes gluey and worthless. Finally, we drain the pasta and toss it with a *condimento*. These actions are like a memory in our bodies. Writing this book, we had to *think* about these things for the first time—about what exactly we were doing and why—so that we could pass this information on to our readers, who may not have pasta running through their blood as we do. In this book we have tried to reveal all the little "tricks," gathered over the years, to help you make every pasta dish a perfect one. But the true and only trick is to cook with passion.

For us, pasta is more than just a food. It is part of our histories. This simple substance, boiled in water and salt, has managed to sustain entire populations in the darkest times of poverty. It is a good friend, a member of the family. It is something we love. While it nourishes the body, it also gives a unique sense of satisfaction and comfort that is so deep, I'm afraid you might think I am crazy if I try to explain it. Though we have a diverse cuisine in Sicily, and all over Italy, it is pasta—in small shapes, like ditalini—that we are weaned on. It is pasta that we are fed when we are sick, and pasta that sustains us when we are old and have neither the teeth nor the digestion for anything else. When we are living well, it is over a plate of pasta that friendships are born and family ties are reinforced. As a matter of habit and history, pasta is what we reach for to comfort ourselves and our loved ones in the happiest of times and the saddest. It is the food we identify ourselves with as Italians and the food we miss most when we travel abroad.

When Italians offer a plate of pasta to friends or strangers, we are opening the doors of our homes and welcoming them inside in the most generous way. It is in that spirit that my mamma and I, who have had the good fortune to be accompanied all our lives by this most versatile of foods, these golden strands of nourishment, invite you through the tall, ancient wooden doors of Gangivecchio and offer up these recipes, these one hundred versions of the golden strands, the god, pasta, to you. So put the water on to boil. And *buon appetito!*

My first memory of pasta is as old as my first memory. When I was a child, forced to stay in bed by the flu, the treatment was to lie under tons of heavy blankets in order to sweat out the illness. After the sweat was over, I would change into a clean set of pajamas my mother had waiting for me on a chair beside my bed. I would jump on the bed, slide under the covers, joyfully moving my feet and fingers, and wait for "pastina," small shapes of pasta used in soup. My mother would put *lingua di passera*, "sparrow's tongue," in broth, and bring it to my mouth. Once she left the room, I got great pleasure letting it dribble down my chin. Those first tastes of pasta are like tastes of my childhood, and still follow me through my life.

In my generation, we wished for many grand things that we knew would never become a reality. But because our dreams were so heartfelt, we were content with just the wish. Everything we had was given to us by our parents, parsimoniously, and we accepted it all with joy. Sometimes, for example, we were allowed to go, a big group of us, for a walk in the country or to the seaside. On those days, we left at dawn, a group of fifteen or twenty boys and girls, weighted down with parcels, blankets, closed baskets of food, and with an old crackling gramophone and as many opera records as we could carry. After setting down our things and spreading out our blankets, we put on *Aida*, like a triumphal march, and broke out the timballos our mothers had prepared for us. We ate our own and tasted everyone else's. It was like a competition, but we all declared that our own mother's timballos were the best.

Like a spy before those picnics, I watched my mamma in the kitchen, preparing the sauces that would be mixed together, boiling the maccheroni, and pressing it all into the pan. But I didn't begin to cook until I arrived at Gangivecchio fifty-six years ago. I was a young woman, deeply in love, ready to live life as an adventure. A city girl, I had come to live with my new husband in the house that belonged to his family, in the middle of nowhere.

It was here, in the country, that I learned there was another reality, a way of living, of poverty and hunger, so far from what I knew. In the beginning, I was astonished at the way my husband and his parents accepted the state of things. It was as if they could not even imagine a more civil and comfortable way of life for those families who were working for them. The servants shared small spaces with animals, with roofs so low that it was impossible to stand up straight. There were no bathrooms, and to heat the house, there was only a big pan boiling over a smoky fire night and day. The men looked double their age, the women trusted only God for their survival, and the sick children hadn't any idea of education or school. Pasta was their only food, and it was their salvation.

At that time, there were a few food shops in Gangi, the small town near our house, each of which sold pasta, not in colored paper packages, as we see today. The two most common shapes, spaghetti and ditalini, were stored in a big wooden drawer behind the counter. When you told the shopkeeper what you wanted, he took it out of the drawer, weighed it, and wrapped it in deep blue, rustic paper. It was difficult then, with no cars and only horses, to go the few miles from the country into town. So when we did, we bought a large amount, enough to feed our families for a couple of weeks.

Pasta was the cheapest thing you could buy. The people of Gangi bought as much as they could afford, and cooked it in a big pan on a wood-burning stove (the one that also served as the central heating for the house). They tossed the pasta with a simple tomato sauce or greens, like borage and chard, that grow wild in the mountains here. The point of the pasta was that it nourished them, and that it was enough to fill the stomach for several hours. So I suppose it is to the peasant class that we owe the heralded "Mediterranean Diet." The irony is not lost on the peasants. Years ago, one of our workers, an old man, told me: "I am sure that the first doctor who spoke of the Mediterranean Diet was sated with meat and sausages."

Here at Gangivecchio, I learned to cook from my husband's mother, and from my heart, as I cooked to feed my husband and children. In the beginning, Granny, as my children called her, would cook all the meals. She didn't allow anybody in her kitchen. But slowly she began to let me watch, and then to teach me. She became like a mother to me, and taught me to make many of the classic Sicilian dishes, like *pasta con le sarde*, in the old-fashioned way.

Many of the recipes in this book are those she taught me, passed on from one generation to another. Many are classics of Sicily. Many I made for my husband to re-create dishes we discovered on trips to the seaside or at a wonderful restaurant in Palermo. Many are those favorites that I make especially for my son, Paolo, others especially for my daughter, Giovanna. And many are those I invented playing in the kitchen as I do every day, cooking for our guests at the restaurant on Sundays, for Peppe, Mariano, Loredana, and the others who work for us, cooking for our beloved cats and dogs every day. My kitchen is my home; it is the place where I express my creativity and my love. And with these recipes, I open up that place to you.

All the recipes in this book, as in our two previous books, *La Cucina Siciliana di Gangivecchio* and *Sicilian Home Cooking*, were born, tested, and tasted here at Gangivecchio, our family home. For those of our readers who haven't read our other books, we want to introduce you to this place that is both the inspiration for our cooking and the protagonist of our writing.

Gangivecchio, which means "old Gangi," is a former Benedictine abbey of the fourteenth century, nestled on a hillside in the Madonie Mountains, about two hours by car from Palermo and two miles from the medieval town of Gangi. Gangivecchio was abandoned by the monks at the end of the sixteenth century. After a long period of loneliness, Gangivecchio became a private property. And for the last 150 years it has belonged to our family. It is not just our home, of course—now it is a restaurant and an inn. As we often say, we do not own this place; this place owns us. Gangivecchio drives our lives and our desires. It is the place where we have our roots, where we live, and where we work, often with joy, and always with the feeling that we have chosen the right life by living here.

To be truthful, it was in order to maintain this place financially that we invented a restaurant in the west wing of the abbey. But we like to think that it was the answer to a whispering desire of these walls that we have returned Gangivecchio to the ways of the ancient monks, welcoming and nourishing those who knock at our door.

It is only natural that a pasta book should be born of this place. You can imagine, through the centuries, how many dishes of pasta have been cooked, dressed, and eaten at Gangivecchio, starting from the big common plates of the monks, to the big wooden dishes of the workers, eaten in the large, dark, smoky dining room on the first floor of the abbey, where the only light was a candle. Perhaps it was a comforting bowl of soup with ditalini, or a masterpiece of homemade ziti tossed with a meat gravy sauce, perfumed with cinnamon, dusted with grated pecorino, and embellished by chicken kidneys and béchamel. To finish, my mind flies to more recent meals at Gangivecchio: a dish of spaghetti bright with red tomato sauce and a fresh basil leaf, *anelletti al forno* brought out for a picnic, or ravioli glistening in melted butter sauce on the Christmas table.

100 Ways to Be Pasta

Pasta Lessons

When we began writing this book, our new coauthor, Carolina, came to stay with us at Gangivecchio in order to see how we cook—and especially how we cook pasta. As she spent time with us in the kitchen, she was constantly asking us: "Why are you doing this? Why did you just do that?" Sometimes we would give her the real answer, other times we would tell her, "Everyone knows that!" But, of course, what we really meant is that every Italian knows that. Even after writing two books, we were astonished at how many things we do in making pasta that others are not accustomed to doing. If we didn't believe her then, we did after watching an American cooking show on television one morning. What we saw was so unbelievable that when Carolina came to the house, we asked her: Is it true? That Americans throw a string of spaghetti against the wall? The man on the show said that this is how Americans test pasta: if it sticks, it is done. She said, yes, it is true. We howled with a combination of horror and hilarity, imagining cooks all over America throwing spaghetti against their kitchen walls. To keep all of your walls clean and pasta-free, see the following pages for our short lesson on pasta. And throughout the book, we give you all our little "tricks" that make pasta in Sicily, and in Italy, so good. Of course, you must remember that the only real trick to making good food is passion.

CHOOSING A PASTA SHAPE

We Italians have more shapes for pasta than you can imagine. Pasta fills an entire aisle of the grocery store. We all have giant larders or drawers filled with bags of different shapes of pasta. We can have forty or a hundred bags and still go to the store for more if we do not have the exact right shape. If we call for a particular shape in one recipe and you cannot find it, use a similar shape, or one with the same qualities. Short pasta shapes are used when you want to be able to stab the food with a fork, as you would if you had cut vegetables or meat in a pasta. Long thin strands, like spaghetti and linguine, are used with light, slippery sauces that will coat them. A rich, creamy sauce often wants a wide and substantial pasta shape, like pappardelle or festonate; otherwise the sauce will drown the pasta. Pasta with holes, like penne and rigatoni, hold ingredients inside them, if the ingredients are small, like peas or ground meat. And the grooves on the outside of *rigate*, "ridged" pastas, help to hold a sauce.

COOKING PASTA

The first thing you do when you cook pasta is fill a pot with water. Remember, don't use too much. You need about 1 gallon of water for 1 pound of pasta. Then you salt the water. For long pasta, we add oil. Otherwise not. We always stir the pasta when we put it in the water, and again while it is cooking—especially long strands, but no pasta wants to be ignored. The most important thing when cooking pasta is to check on it frequently. If you ignore it, you will overcook it. For an Italian, this is unacceptable. We absolutely cannot eat overcooked pasta.

A FISTFUL OF SALT

When we originally wrote our recipes, we wrote to "salt the water to taste." Then we learned that many Americans are in the habit of salting the pasta water with a few dashes of the shaker in a big pot of water. Pasta water should taste like broth. It should have the amount of salty taste in it that you want for the finished pasta dish. We have a big jar of Sicilian sea salt next to our stove and scoop up *un pugnetto*, "a small fist-ful," to put in the pot of water. Then we taste the broth to see that it has enough salt, and we add more if necessary as the pasta is cooking. We never, ever, salt a pasta dish after it has been tossed with the *condimento*. Then you can feel the salt on the food, and that is all you can taste. By salting the water, the salt gets in the pasta and brings out the flavor.

TENDER VS. AL DENTE

We have two words for cooking pasta: tender and al dente. Al dente means "to the tooth." It refers to pasta that is cooked so you can still feel it under your teeth, really bite into it. Tender is cooked just slightly longer. The only pastas that we Tornabenes like to eat al dente are the long thin shapes, like spaghetti, linguine, and fettuccine. The others, we cook until tender. That said, we know that Americans have a tendency to overcook pasta. It would make us very happy to be sure you know that "tender" does not mean mushy!

HOLY PASTA WATER

One thing that makes a good pasta is the texture. It should be wet and slippery, not dry and sticky. The *condimento* must coat the pasta perfectly, and what makes that possible is using pasta water. Some pasta dishes, like a simple oil and garlic pasta, demand more pasta water than others, but there is not a single pasta that we make that we do not add pasta water to. We would never use another water—the pasta water has starch in it from the pasta, and it is salty. It is integral to the dish. So never forget to save some pasta water before draining the pasta, or after the pasta is removed from the pot. You will find it very helpful.

DRAINING PASTA

Draining pasta has its own rhythm in our cooking. We do it two ways. In the case of long strands, like spaghetti and linguine, we use a *scola spaghetti*, a spaghetti strainer, to lift the pasta out of the water and into the bowl or pot with the *condimento*. We don't drain these long strands through a colander because they have a tendency to stick together if you do. In the case of hollow tubes or short pastas, we drain the pasta quickly through a colander in the sink. In either case, the time from the pasta leaving the water to the time it reaches the *condimento* happens in seconds. We do not try to get all the water out; a little dripping water is good for the *condimento*, and we will be adding more hot pasta water anyway. We have seen some people—not Italians!—drain pasta in a colander in the sink. And then they let it sit there and sit there until they are ready to serve it. We have also heard that some people rinse pasta after it is cooked. After either of these crimes, the pasta is sure to have lost all its life.

SERVING PASTA

The most important thing to us when making and serving pasta is that almost no time pass between when the pasta is tossed, when it is set on the table, and when the first person reaches into the bowl to serve himself. After all, pasta that is steaming hot is a beautiful thing to see and to eat. Pasta that has been sitting for five minutes first gets cold. Then it begins to turn to something else: glue. It is a ritual that we have everything else ready before the pasta is put in the water: the table is set, everyone is around the table waiting to eat, the cheese is on the table, the wine is poured, and the only thing left to do is boil the pasta. Just before the pasta is served, you will hear the words in any Italian house: "*A tavola!*" "To the table!" This means the pasta is almost ready. Better that you wait for the pasta than that the pasta waits for you. When everything is all set, we put the bowl of pasta to our left, serve ourselves, and quickly pass it along.

"When you use your hands to make food, you transfer the love from your hands to the food. Also, the hands are warm, just the right temperature for working with dough."
—G.

Fresh Pasta Dough

Makes about 1 1/2 pounds of pasta

6 cups all–purpose flour
6 small eggs
1 1/2 tablespoons olive oil
1 teaspoon salt

Mound the flour into a hill on your work surface. Create a hole in the middle. Break the eggs into the hole, and add the oil and salt. Using the tips of your fingers, work the eggs into the flour from the outer walls inward. Continue mixing to form a dough. Lightly flour your work surface, shape the dough into a ball, and knead it until it is smooth and silky, adding more flour if the dough gets sticky. This will take about 10 minutes. Divide the dough in half. Roll each half into a ball and press into a flat disk. Cover and refrigerate for 1 hour. Roll through a pasta maker or roll with a rolling pin. Cut into thin strips or make ravioli (page 100).

TIP Use only cold water when making homemade pasta dough. Otherwise you will get lumps.

We always knead pasta dough by hand. This way, we can feel when the dough has come together just right.

Fresh Tomato Sauce

Makes about 2 quarts

Fresh tomato sauce is the base of much of our cooking. In the summertime, when we harvest tomatoes from our garden, we hire a woman here in the countryside who makes fresh tomato sauce from them and bottles it for us. She takes half the bottles as payment, and we are left with a larder full of sauce, to use throughout the year. When we see so many bottles lined up, it is impossible to believe that we could ever run out— but we always do. And then we make fresh tomato sauce dish by dish, as we need it. We use good canned Italian tomatoes, since by the time we run out, tomatoes are out of season. Making fresh tomato sauce is a simple process, something that comes so naturally to us, we could do it in our sleep. Specialty stores in America have recently begun importing bottled fresh tomato sauce from Italy. You'll usually find it in tall bottles, like our water bottles. It is different from supermarket pasta sauces, which are cooked longer and are therefore thicker, and have added seasoning.

We add dried oregano, not fresh, to our tomato sauce.

1. Combine the tomatoes, onions, and basil together with the water in a large pot. Season with salt and cook over medium heat for about 15 minutes, stirring often.

2. Pass the tomato sauce through a food mill. Return the sauce to the pot you cooked it in. Add the olive oil, whole basil leaves, sugar, and salt and pepper to taste. Simmer for 30 minutes, stirring occasionally. Adjust the salt, pepper, and sugar to taste.

5 pounds fresh tomatoes, cored and chopped (or four 28–ounce cans peeled whole Italian tomatoes, drained in a colander and broken up with your hands)

1 large white or yellow onion, chopped

1 bunch fresh basil leaves, chopped (about 1/2 cup), plus 6 whole basil leaves

4 cups water

1/2 cup olive oil

1 tablespoon sugar (or more to taste)

Salt and freshly ground black pepper

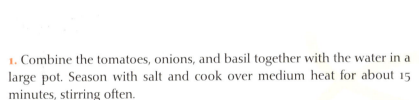

Soffritto can refer to anything with olive oil, garlic, and onions in a frying pan. The mixture of carrots, celery, onions, and garlic is the classic Italian *soffritto* and the base of many Italian dishes.

Condimento comes from the word *condire*, which means to mix or to dress, as in to dress the pasta with whatever you choose. This can be any topping for a pasta that is not "sauce." Sauce means one thing and only one thing: tomato sauce. *Condiamo la pasta* means "Let's dress the pasta." In other words, it's time to toss it with the *condimento* and eat!

Scola spaghetti is the tool we use to pick spaghetti strands out of the pot. You call it a spaghetti strainer.

Sformato means "turned out." A timballo that has been flipped over and out onto a platter is a *sformato*.

Al dente means "to the teeth." We use this phrase to refer to pasta that is cooked until it is just before tender, so you can feel it on your teeth. This is the way we prefer spaghetti and linguine.

Pugnetto means a small fistful. It is how we measure many things, especially salt.

Un ciuffo is a word we use in the kitchen for leafy herbs, such as basil, oregano, mint, marjoram, parsley, and sage. It means a small bunch, like the way you would carry the herbs or flowers back from the garden. We also use this to describe the part of your hair that you let fall over your face. You can also use the word *ciuffetto*, which simply means a small *ciuffo*.

Ragù is any mixture of meat or ground meat cooked in a frying pan with olive oil and other ingredients, like *soffritto*, for a long time. We often add tomato sauce to *ragù*, but not always.

Una noce di burro, "a walnut of butter," is a very loose measurement that refers to the size of an unshelled walnut. The equivalent is about 2 tablespoons.

Butta giù la pasta! means "Put on the pasta!" These are the words we yell from the dining room to the kitchen. It means that the table is set, everyone is ready, so start cooking the pasta. All the activity in the kitchen and of those who are eating is planned around the pasta. There must be no time between when the steaming bowl of pasta is set down on the table and when the first person begins to serve from it.

Pirofila is what we call a baking dish that you can put in the oven and that is also nice enough to put on the table. We use it for things like lasagne that must be served straight from the pan.

Legare la salsa means to "tighten the sauce." The meaning of "tight" is a little different when you use it in the kitchen. It means to bring the sauce together so it is creamy rather than runny. Usually this means adding some flour and cooking it longer. If you cook it too long and it needs "loosening," we say *restringere la salsa*.

Ravioli is one of the few pastas we make by hand. Making ravioli takes all morning and many hands.

Quick and Easy Pastas
(Pasta Sbrigativa!)

1. Quick Spicy Pennette with Anchovies and Buffalo Mozzarella
   (Pennette Sbrigativa con Acciughe e Mozzarella di Bufala)

2. Farfalle with Sweet Green Peas and Prosciutto Cotto *(Farfalle Verdi)*

3. Gnocchetti with Sweet Peppers and Cherry Tomatoes
   (Gnocchetti con Peperoni e Pomodori)

4. Simple Midnight Spaghetti with Garlic, Oil, and Hot Pepper
   (Spaghetti di Mezzanotte con Aglio, Olio e Peperoncino)

5. Fiery Spaghetti with Anchovies, Olives, and Capers in a Quick Tomato
   Sauce *(Un Saporito Piatto di Fuoco)*

6. Gobbetti with Fresh Ricotta, Gruyère, and Nutmeg
   (Gobbetti con Ricotta Fresca, Groviera e Noce)

7. Spaghetti with Raw Tomato, Garlic, and Basil *(Pesto di Trapani)*

8. Spaghetti with Tomatoes and Pancetta from Amatrice
   (Spaghetti all'Amatriciana)

9. Bucatini with Pancetta, Smoked Provola Cheese, and Peperoncino
   (Bucatini Affumicati)

10. Paolo's Summer Fettuccine with Crème Fraîche and Orange Zest
    (*Fettuccine Estive di Paolo con Panna e Scorza d'Arancia*)

11. Giovanna's Tagliatelle with Tuna and Curry
    (*Le Tagliatelle di Giovanna con Tonno e Curry*)

12. Alda's Pastasciutta with Green Beans and Pecorino
    (*Pastasciutta e Fagiolini di Alda*)

13. Sedanini with Ricotta, Saffron, and Rosemary (*Sedanini con Ricotta e Zafferano*)

14. Tagliatelline with Zucchini Flowers and Fresh Herbs
    (*Tagliatelline con Fiori di Zucca*)

15. Classic Spaghetti with Tuna Roe (*Classici Spaghetti alla Bottarga*)

16. Agrigento-Style Garlic and Oil Spaghetti with Saffron
    (*Spaghetti Aglio e Olio di Agrigento*)

17. Mezze Maniche with Sun-Dried Tomatoes and Green Olives
    (*Mezze Maniche con Pomodori Secchi*)

18. Tagliolini with Green Apple Pesto and Speck (*Tagliolini con Mela Verdi e Speck*)

19. Cavatelli with Arugula and Pecorino (*Cavatelli con Rucola e Pecorino*)

20. Spaghetti Carbonara (*Spaghetti alla Carbonara*)

21. Pink Spaghetti with Anchovies and Breadcrumbs
    (*Spaghetti con Acciughe e Mollica Rossa*)

22. Linguine with Scallions, Raisins, and Turmeric
    (*Linguine con lo Scalogno e Curcuma*)

23. Tagliatelle with Fresh Tomato and Garlic (*Tagliatelle con Salsa Picchio Pacchio*)

24. Quick Tagliatelle with Fried Zucchini and Parsley
    (*Pasta Veloce con Zucchine e Prezzemolo*)

*I*n Italian, sbrigativa *doesn't just mean "quick." Quick is just the best trans-lation we could find. But sbrigativa refers to the way you do things when you have many things to do at the same time. This pasta is the kind of thing we make on such a day. It is the kind of pasta for which the first thing we do is boil the water. Everything else is done in the time it takes for the water to boil and the pasta to cook.*

Farfalle with Sweet Green Peas and Prosciutto Cotto

TIP Add a splash of water whenever you hear something sizzling in the pan.

Quick Spicy Pennette with Anchovies and Buffalo Mozzarella
Pennette Sbrigativa con Acciughe e Mozzarella di Bufala

Serves 6

This is a simple and quick-to-make pasta, an alternative to the basic pasta aglio e olio, *with the added flavor of the anchovies and the gooey melted cheese.*

1 pound pennette lisce (short tubes, smooth, without ridges on the outside)
Salt
12 tablespoons (1 1/2 sticks) unsalted butter
1 tablespoon olive oil
8 anchovy fillets in oil
Pinch of freshly ground black pepper
Pinch of cayenne pepper or hot pepper flakes
1/2 cup (about 1 1/2 ounces) grated Parmesan cheese, plus more for passing at the table
12 ounces buffalo mozzarella, cut into 1/4–inch cubes
2 tablespoons finely chopped fresh Italian parsley

1. Bring a large saucepan of water to a boil. Stir in a small fistful of salt. Add the pennette and cook until tender.
2. Meanwhile, melt the butter and oil together in a large frying pan over very low heat. Add the anchovies, smash them with a fork, and sauté until they dissolve into the oil.
3. Reserve a cupful of the pasta water and drain the pennette quickly in a colander. Add the drained pennette to the pan with the *condimento* and toss very quickly over high heat. Add enough pasta water so that the pasta is slippery, not dry or sticky. Stir in the pepper, hot pepper, and the Parmesan cheese. Turn off the heat. Add the mozzarella cubes, toss, and transfer the pasta to a serving bowl. Dust with more Parmesan cheese and parsley and serve immediately, with Parmesan on the table.

TIP Be careful not to put too much salt in this dish. There is already a lot of salt in the *condimento* because of the anchovies.

Farfalle with Sweet Green Peas and Prosciutto Cotto
Farfalle Verdi

Serves 6

We used to grow our own peas here at Gangivecchio, back when there was someone to shell them. But times have changed. Now we have a smaller staff, women all over Italy are working outside the home, even grannies are not grannies anymore; they are going off to play tennis or find a boyfriend. Once they were staying home, taking care of the children, and shelling peas and beans. Nowadays, we use only frozen peas. This dish is the sort of pasta that the middle class thinks is very elegant, perhaps because with butterflies and peas, it seems light. And the flavors are subtle, especially for those who are used to heavier dishes with tomatoes and onions.

1. Bring a large saucepan of water to a boil. Stir in a small fistful of salt and the farfalle and boil until the pasta is tender.

2. While the pasta is cooking, melt the butter with a tablespoon or two of water in a large frying pan over low heat. Add the scallions and sauté them for a minute or two, until they soften. Add the peas, ham, and salt and pepper to taste, and a small ladleful of hot pasta water, and cook until the peas are tender. Add a splash more hot pasta water as you're cooking if the vegetables are sticking to the pan. Taste for salt and pepper. Keep warm, and when the pasta is almost done, transfer to a pasta bowl.

3. Reserve a cupful of the pasta water and drain the pasta quickly in a colander. Turn the pasta into the serving bowl on top of the peas and scallion *condimento*. Toss, adding a splash of hot pasta water if necessary. Sprinkle with the Parmesan cheese, and serve hot with more Parmesan at the table.

"For me, boiling water is a comforting thing. When the water is boiling, it means I'm halfway through, and I'm about to sit down with my pasta. Especially when I'm alone in the kitchen: the water starts to boil and even if I don't put the pasta in yet, the sound of the boiling water is like having company in the kitchen."

—G.

1 pound farfalle
8 tablespoons (1 stick) unsalted butter
1 scallion, minced (white part only)
1/2 pound frozen petite green peas
1/4 pound prosciutto cotto (boiled ham), cut into 1/2–inch cubes
Salt and freshly ground black pepper
1/2 cup (about 1 1/2 ounces) freshly grated Parmesan cheese, plus more for passing at the table

Gnocchetti with Sweet Peppers and Cherry Tomatoes
Gnocchetti con Peperoni e Pomodori

Serves 4

GNOCCHETTI

is shaped like gnocchi, the fresh semolina dumplings, only they are smaller, and dried. They are famous as a pasta that takes a long time to cook. We often call them "Sardinian gnocchetti," because they have a shape that is very common on that island.

This is a recipe from my friend Catarina. Last summer, she and I went on a hike to a natural reserve called Zingaro (which means "Gypsy") on the western coast of Sicily near the town of Castellamare. It's beautiful, absolutely wild. You can only get there by walking; there are no roads, no cars. Catarina has a little house there just on the sea. We had to cook for ourselves, five people in all. First we had a swim in the sea, and then we made a pasta with what we had all brought. This area is now a wildlife reserve, so the only other people who live there are those that already had small, simple country houses before it was forbidden to build. It's the most incredible place in that there is absolutely no noise. You hear only the sea, the water on the rocks, the birds, and the wind.

1 red bell pepper
1 green bell pepper
1 yellow bell pepper
Salt
3/4 pound gnocchetti
1/2 cup extra virgin olive oil
1 small white or yellow onion, sliced
1 garlic clove, thinly sliced
1/2 pound cherry tomatoes, halved
4 anchovy fillets in oil
Freshly ground black pepper
1/2 cup finely chopped fresh Italian parsley
Freshly grated Parmesan cheese

1. Preheat the oven to 450°F.

2. Rinse the peppers and place them directly on the oven grill with a pan or sheet of foil underneath to catch the liquids. Roast the peppers, turning them occasionally, until they are black on all sides. Remove the peppers from the oven and place them in a paper or plastic bag covered with a damp paper towel to steam for 10 to 15 minutes. Skin the peppers. Cut them in half, remove the cores and seeds, and cut into thin strips.

3. Bring a large saucepan of water to a boil. Stir in a small fistful of salt. Add the gnocchetti and cook until the pasta is tender.

4. While the pasta is cooking, heat the oil in a large frying pan over medium heat. Add the onions and sauté for 3 to 4 minutes, until they are tender and translucent. Add the garlic slices and sauté for about 2 minutes, until they are light golden, but be careful not to let them brown. Add the cherry tomatoes, the pepper strips, the anchovies, and salt and pepper to taste, and sauté until the anchovies have dissolved into the oil. Turn off the heat.

5. Reserve a cupful of the pasta water and drain the gnocchetti in a colander. Quickly transfer the drained gnocchetti to the pan with the pepper *condimento*, place over high heat, and mix them together, adding pasta water until the pasta is slippery and not dry. Stir in the parsley. Transfer to a serving bowl and serve immediately, with grated Parmesan cheese on the table.

"Stir long pasta with a big long fork. Stir short pastas with a wooden spoon. That's just the way it's done."
—G.

Simple Midnight Spaghetti with Garlic, Oil, and Hot Pepper
Spaghetti di Mezzanotte con Aglio, Olio e Peperoncino

Serves 4

In Italy, we have a nickname for this pasta: "midnight spaghetti." When I was a young girl in Palermo, it was the kind of spaghetti my friends and I would prepare when we came back from dancing or the theater. We would go all together to one person's house just to continue the night and for the pleasure of being together. This spaghetti was the only thing we could even think about preparing—because it is digestible and simple to make and any Italian is sure to have these ingredients at home.

1. Bring a large saucepan of water to a boil. Stir in a small fistful of salt and a splash of olive oil. Add the spaghetti and stir to prevent it from sticking together. Cook the spaghetti, stirring often, until it is al dente.

2. While the pasta is cooking, heat the oil with the minced garlic in a frying pan over medium heat and sauté the garlic for 3 to 5 minutes, until it is very aromatic. Do not let the garlic turn darker than golden brown—turn the heat down if necessary. Season the garlic oil with salt, pepper, and pepper flakes.

3. Use a *scola spaghetti* to lift the spaghetti out of the water and into the frying pan with the garlic oil. Add a generous amount of pasta water and the minced parsley and toss to coat the spaghetti, adding more pasta water until the pasta is slippery and not sticky or dry. Transfer the spaghetti to a serving bowl. Sprinkle with grated Parmesan cheese and serve immediately, with more cheese at the table.

"You could cut long pasta instead of trying to twirl it all onto your fork or slurping the last bit. But for Italians to cut long pasta, it's like a surrender. We would never do this. Never."

—G.

1/2 pound spaghetti
Salt
1/2 cup extra virgin olive oil, plus more for the pasta water
3 garlic cloves, minced
Freshly ground black pepper
Pinch of hot pepper flakes
2 tablespoons finely chopped fresh Italian parsley
Freshly grated Parmesan cheese

"I like to cook alone. I like to concentrate. I can only stand one person to help: Peppe. Because he is there to wash and clean after me. And to peel the garlic so my fingers don't smell like garlic."

—W.

"It is not elegant to twirl your spaghetti on a spoon."
—W.

Fiery Spaghetti with Anchovies, Olives, and Capers in a Quick Tomato Sauce
Un Saporito Piatto di Fuoco

Serves 6

The meeting of anchovies, black olives, and peppers is a classic of the Sicilian kitchen. We always use capers packed in salt. If you rinse them, you can get rid of the salt and you're left with the taste of the capers. With the capers in vinegar, even if you rinse them, you're left with the taste of the vinegar.

One 16-ounce can peeled whole tomatoes, drained in a colander
3/4 cup extra virgin olive oil, plus more for the pasta water
2 garlic cloves, peeled and smashed
8 anchovy fillets in oil
2 tablespoons capers in salt, rinsed and minced
3 tablespoons black olives, pitted and chopped
One 2-inch hot red pepper, halved and seeds removed
Salt
1/2 cup finely chopped fresh Italian parsley
1 pound spaghetti
Freshly grated Parmesan cheese

1. If you are using canned whole tomatoes, pour them in a colander placed in the sink to drain for at least 15 minutes.

2. Warm the olive oil with the smashed garlic cloves in a large frying pan over low heat and sauté the garlic for a few minutes until it is very aromatic and light golden. Add the anchovies, smash them with the back of a fork, and sauté until the anchovy pieces have dissolved. Add the capers, olives, and the halved hot pepper and sauté for a few minutes, until the pepper is soft.

3. Squish the tomatoes between your fingers directly into the frying pan. Add salt to taste and cook over medium heat for about 20 minutes, until all the ingredients are integrated and very thick. You may need to add a little water if the mixture starts to stick to the pan. Stir in the parsley, taste again for salt, and turn off the heat until you're ready to toss the *condimento* with the pasta.

4. In the meantime, bring a large saucepan of water to a boil. Stir in a small fistful of salt and a splash of oil. Add the spaghetti and stir to prevent it from sticking together. Boil until the spaghetti is al dente. Lift the spaghetti out of the pot, reserving the pasta water, and place in the frying pan with the *condimento*. Toss the spaghetti with the *condimento* and a small ladleful of hot pasta water over high heat for 2 minutes, adding more hot pasta water if the spaghetti is dry or sticky. Transfer the spaghetti to a pasta bowl and serve immediately with grated Parmesan cheese.

Gobbetti with Fresh Ricotta, Gruyère, and Nutmeg
Gobbetti con Ricotta Fresca, Groviera e Noce

Serves 6

This is a very simple pasta dish, and one that relies on the quality of fresh ricotta. In Gangi, fresh sheep's ricotta is something you buy and use the day it is made. It is very delicate. We know you probably don't have the luxury of finding this cheese down the road from your home, but we have learned that there are some cheese makers in America making fresh ricotta—some even from sheep's milk. As for the nutmeg, of course ground works in place of freshly grated, but because the flavors of this dish are so subtle, we think the fresh nutmeg makes a difference.

1. Bring a large saucepan of water to a boil. Stir in a small fistful of salt. Add the gobbetti and cook, stirring occasionally until the pasta is tender.
2. While the pasta is cooking, melt the butter and oil together in a large saucepan over medium heat. Add the sieved ricotta and the milk and stir with a wooden spoon to mix well. Lower the heat and stir in the Gruyère. Stir in salt, pepper, and nutmeg and taste, adding more of any of them if necessary. Cook for about 5 minutes over low heat until the Gruyère is melted and the sauce is creamy.
3. When the pasta is ready, reserve a cupful of the pasta water and drain the pasta quickly in a colander. Add the pasta and a little bit of pasta water to the frying pan with the cheese sauce and cook over very high heat for about 2 minutes. Add more pasta water if the pasta is sticky. Transfer the pasta to a pasta bowl and serve with freshly grated Parmesan.

TIP You don't want to drain pasta so much that it won't drip. A little bit of hot water on the pasta helps the *condimento* coat it and keeps it from being dry. If you need to, carry the pot you cooked it in underneath the colander to catch the water that might drip.

GOBBETTI
means "little hunchbacks," and that describes the shape of this pasta. It is not the most often used shape, but it cooks quickly, is easy to eat, and is good to have around for a last-minute pasta.

1 pound gobbetti
8 tablespoons (1 stick) unsalted butter
1 tablespoon olive oil
1 pound fresh ricotta,* passed through a fine silk screen or sieve
1/2 cup milk
1/2 cup grated Gruyère cheese
Salt and freshly ground black pepper
1/2 teaspoon freshly grated nutmeg
Freshly grated Parmesan cheese

See source list.

Spaghetti with Raw Tomato, Garlic, and Basil
Pesto di Trapani

Serves 6

3 garlic cloves, minced
10 fresh basil leaves, torn into
  small pieces
Salt
4 fresh tomatoes, peeled, seeded,
  and coarsely chopped
1/2 cup almonds, toasted and finely
  chopped
Pinch of cayenne pepper or hot
  pepper flakes
Freshly ground black pepper
1/2 cup (or more) extra virgin olive
  oil, plus more for the pasta water
1 pound spaghetti

"Slurping spaghetti at dinner is like picking your nose at a party."

—W.

This pasta comes from Trapani, a town on the west coast of Sicily where they often use garlic as the main ingredient. It is a summertime pasta that must start with very ripe, sweet tomatoes. The condimento *is not cooked, but the ingredients marinate together for at least a couple of hours and as long as two days. The almonds sprinkled over the finished dish remind us of the ancient Arabian domination of that part of the island. It might seem unusual; we think it will be the perfect pasta for you to enjoy on a warm summer afternoon, just as we do.*

1. Crush the garlic, basil, and a pinch of salt with a mortar and pestle until they form a paste. Add the tomatoes, half of the almonds, the hot pepper, and salt and pepper to taste. Transfer the paste to a pasta bowl and add the oil slowly until it forms a loose, creamy pesto. Let rest, covered, at room temperature for at least two hours, preferably overnight.
2. Bring a large saucepan of water to a boil. Stir in a small fistful of salt and a splash of olive oil. Add the spaghetti and stir immediately to prevent it from sticking together. Boil until the pasta is al dente. Meanwhile, ladle 1/2 cup of hot pasta water into the bowl with the *condimento*. Lift the pasta out of the water and into the bowl with the *condimento* using a spaghetti strainer. Add a splash more pasta water and mix well, adding more pasta water if necessary. Sprinkle with the remaining almonds and serve immediately.

TIP Basil was once thought a holy plant. Women, who were considered inferior beings, were forbidden to touch it. Today, basil is used to keep away mosquitoes. You can see bunches of basil in the windows of houses in town.

TO PEEL TOMATOES, bring a large saucepan of water to a boil. Carve an "X" in the top of each tomato with a small knife. Drop the tomatoes into the water and boil them for about **1** minute, until the skin at the "X" begins to curl back. Remove the tomatoes from the water with a slotted spoon. When they are cool enough to touch, use the knife to peel back and remove the skin. Cut the tomatoes in half, spoon out the seeds, and proceed with your recipe.

OPPOSITE: *In the summertime, ripe tomatoes and sweet peppers are a constant inspiration.*

Spaghetti with Tomatoes and Pancetta from Amatrice
Spaghetti all'Amatriciana

Serves 6

The name of this pasta comes from the town of Amatrice, where it is their traditional dish. There, they use guanciale, which is a sort of prosciutto that is very fatty. We use pancetta in its place. Many people add cream to pasta all'Amatriciana. *But never do this. It's terrible. It becomes a very heavy dish, which is a mistake, as the beauty of this recipe is that it is quick, simple, and flavorful—without being rich.*

1. Heat the oil in a large frying pan over medium heat. Add the pancetta and sauté until it is golden brown, about 5 minutes. Add the wine and cook for a minute to let the alcohol evaporate. Add the tomatoes, red pepper flakes, and salt to taste and continue to cook for about 15 minutes, until the tomatoes have broken down.

2. Meanwhile, bring a large saucepan of water to a boil. Stir in a small fistful of salt and a splash of oil. Stir in the spaghetti and cook, stirring occasionally, until it is al dente. Lift the spaghetti out of the water and into the frying pan with the tomatoes. Toss the pasta with the *condimento* over medium–high heat for about 1 minute to heat through. Transfer to a serving bowl, sprinkle with the pecorino cheese, and serve immediately, with more pecorino at the table.

TIP If a dish is *morbida*, it means it looks dry or fuzzy, like a pashmina. When the tomatoes or any *condimento* look *morbida*, they need more oil.

"You know you need to add some hot pasta water to the bowl when you go to pick up a strand of spaghetti and the whole bowl of spaghetti comes with it."

—G.

1/3 cup extra virgin olive oil, plus more for the pasta water
1/4 pound pancetta (or bacon), cut into 1/2-inch cubes
Splash of dry white wine (2 to 3 tablespoons)
2 medium ripe tomatoes, peeled
Pinch of hot pepper flakes
Salt
1 pound spaghetti
1/3 cup (about 1 ounce) freshly grated pecorino cheese, plus more for passing at the table

SPAGHETTI

Spago means "string," so the word *spaghetti* means "lots of little strings." After all the different shapes that we have invented for pasta, spaghetti must be everybody's favorite. We imagine spaghetti are tender strings that tie us together with family, friends, and beloved companions.

8 tablespoons (1 stick) unsalted butter

1/2 cup extra virgin olive oil, plus more for the pasta water

1 medium white or yellow onion, minced

1 garlic clove, minced

1/2 pound pancetta (or bacon), cut into 1/2-inch cubes

One 1-inch piece of peperoncino (fresh red hot pepper), halved and seeded

One 28-ounce can peeled whole tomatoes, drained in a colander and broken up with your hands

1 tablespoon sugar (or more to taste)

Salt

1 pound bucatini

1/2 pound smoked provola cheese, cut into 1/4-inch matchsticks

1/2 cup (about 1 1/2 ounces) freshly grated Parmesan cheese, plus more for passing at the table

2 tablespoons finely chopped fresh Italian parsley

"Peperoncino is the little fresh hot red pepper that we sometimes add to a soffritto. But peperoncina—with an 'a'—is also used to describe some girls when they are very, you know ... hot!"

—G.

Caciocavallo, a mild semi-hard cheese that is often smoked, can add wonderful flavor to pasta dishes.

Bucatini with Pancetta, Smoked Provola Cheese, and Peperoncino
Bucatini Affumicati

Serves 6

This is a simple, easy-to-make pasta. Made with pancetta and smoked provola cheese, it is a little sweet, a little fiery, and very smoky. If you can find smoked pancetta or smoked bacon, use that.

1. Melt the butter with the oil in a large saucepan over low heat. Add the onions, garlic, and pancetta and sauté 3 to 5 minutes, until the onions soften and the pancetta is golden, making sure not to let the garlic brown. Add the peperoncino, tomatoes, sugar, salt, and 2 tablespoons of water and cook for 20 minutes. Add a splash of water from time to time if you hear the mixture sizzling or see it sticking to the pan. Taste for sugar and salt and add more if you like. Remove the pepper so no one will get a tongue scalding.

2. Meanwhile, bring a large saucepan of water to a boil. Stir in a small fistful of salt, a splash of oil, and the bucatini and boil, stirring often with a long fork to make sure the long pasta strands don't stick together, until the pasta is tender. Reserve some of the hot pasta water and drain the pasta through a colander.

3. Quickly transfer the drained pasta to the saucepan with the *condimento*. Add a splash of pasta water and stir the pasta with the *condimento* together over high heat, adding more pasta water if the pasta is sticky rather than slippery. Add the provola and Parmesan cheese and cook over high heat for 1 to 2 minutes, stirring constantly. Transfer to a serving dish. Sprinkle with the minced parsley and serve immediately with grated Parmesan on the table.

BUCATINI, which literally means "little bucato" (bucato is another pasta shape), is the shape of pasta that we use with both of our classic pasta dishes—pasta with sardines and pasta with cauliflower. It is a long, hollow tube, thinner than bucato. It's a difficult pasta to eat—because it is so thick, it is almost impossible to twirl on a fork. If you can't twirl the entire strand, which almost nobody can do and certainly you cannot if you did not grow up doing it, you have to slurp the end into your mouth. If you do this with a pasta covered in *condimento*—and especially one that has a hole in it that is full of *condimento*—at the end of the slurp, some of the *condimento* is sure to fly out. Once, at a formal dinner in a town nearby, they served homemade bucatini with the chef's special *condimento*. Nobody wanted to use their napkin as a shield, so we all went on as if nothing unusual was happening, but everyone had oil and *condimento* all over their shirtfronts. At our family table, my brother, Paolo, always guards himself with his napkin when anybody is slurping bucatini nearby.

At Il Capo, the big market in Palermo, we find chiles and spices that contribute to Sicily's diverse cuisine.

"No matter how long it is, twirling spaghetti on a fork is in our blood. We never, ever cut spaghetti."

—G.

Salt
Olive oil
1 pound fettuccine
Zest of 1 large orange (long julienne pieces of the top orange layer, not the white pith beneath)
1/2 pound crème fraîche
1/4 cup chopped fresh basil leaves
Freshly grated Parmesan cheese

Paolo's Summer Fettuccine with Crème Fraîche and Orange Zest
Fettuccine Estive di Paolo con Panna e Scorza d'Arancia

Serves 6

This pasta is Paolo's creation. He likes to make it when the weather is hot, because the condimento is not even cooked. With the basil and the orange zest, he calls it "a play of scents."

1. Bring a large saucepan of water to a boil. Stir in a small fistful of salt, a splash of oil, and the fettuccine, and cook until the pasta is al dente.
2. Meanwhile, in a separate, small saucepan boil the orange zest just until it is flabby, about 3 minutes.
3. Lift the fettuccine out of the pasta water into a serving bowl. Add the orange zest, crème fraîche, basil, and a splash of pasta water. The pasta should not be dry; if necessary, add more pasta water until it is creamy. Serve immediately, and pass the Parmesan.

Cardoons and blood oranges are two of the natural wonders of Sicily. In the winter and early spring, they are abundant in the markets of Palermo, like Il Capo.

Giovanna's Tagliatelle with Tuna and Curry
Le Tagliatelle di Giovanna con Tonno e Curry

Serves 6

It's a fact that my daughter, Giovanna, loves spices. She loves curry so much I'm not sure she doesn't put it in her coffee! What I am sure of is that this dish, which she invented the night Carolina arrived in Palermo and we began writing this cookbook, is delicious. It is also very quick and convenient, since canned tuna and curry can be kept in your pantry. —W.

"Many Italians do not serve cheese with seafood dishes. In our family, we do. This tagliatelle with tuna and curry, particularly, tastes great with a little bit of Parmesan."

—G.

1. Heat the butter and oil in a frying pan over low heat. Add the garlic cloves and cook over low heat until they are light golden and fragrant, 2 to 3 minutes.

2. Add the drained tuna to the frying pan and use a wooden spoon to smash the tuna chunks into small bits. Add the curry powder, hot pepper, salt to taste, and 2 tablespoons of water and stir. Let the *condimento* simmer for about 5 minutes to allow the flavors to come together. Add a couple more tablespoons of water while it's cooking if the pan is dry. Remove and discard the garlic cloves.

3. In the meantime, bring a large saucepan of water to a boil. Stir in a small fistful of salt, a splash of oil, and the pasta and cook until al dente. Reserve a cupful of the hot pasta water, quickly drain the tagliatelle in a colander, and dump pasta into the pan with the tuna over high heat. Add 1/2 cup of the pasta water and the parsley and stir for a few minutes over very high heat. Add more pasta water if the pasta is sticky. Serve hot. Pass the Parmesan.

12 tablespoons (1 1/2 sticks) unsalted butter
1/2 cup extra virgin olive oil, plus more for the pasta water
4 garlic cloves
Two 6-ounce cans tuna in olive oil, drained
2 tablespoons curry powder
Pinch of cayenne pepper or hot pepper flakes
Salt
1 pound tagliatelle larghe
1 tablespoon finely chopped fresh Italian parsley
Freshly grated Parmesan cheese

Alda's Pastasciutta with Green Beans and Pecorino
Pastasciutta e Fagiolini di Alda

Serves 6

Paolo's girlfriend, Alda, is a very particular eater. She eats only one shape of pasta: spaghetti. And for reasons we don't understand, she doesn't eat eggplant, peppers, zucchini, or cauliflower. Since she adores green beans, when she comes for lunch, we serve green beans.

Salt
1 1/2 pounds fresh green beans, cleaned and trimmed
1/2 cup extra virgin olive oil, plus more for the pasta water
2 garlic cloves
Freshly ground black pepper
1 pound spaghetti
3 ounces (about 1 cup) freshly grated pecorino cheese

"Pastasciutta literally translates as 'dry pasta.' By this we mean that it is pasta without broth. If we say do you want 'un bel piatto di pastasciutta,' this means: Do you want a good plate of pasta, as opposed to pasta in a minestra, or soup."

—G.

1. Bring a large saucepan of water to a boil. Stir in a small fistful of salt and the green beans and boil until tender. Use a handheld strainer to lift the green beans out of the water, and save the water to cook the pasta in.

2. Coarsely chop the green beans into bite-size pieces. Place the chopped green beans in a mixing bowl, add the olive oil, garlic, salt, and pepper, and mix it all together. Let the beans rest for an hour to marinate, mixing them occasionally since the oil will sink to the bottom.

3. Bring the saucepan of water back to a boil. Add more water and more salt if necessary. Stir in a splash of olive oil and the spaghetti and boil, stirring often with a big fork to keep the spaghetti from sticking together, until al dente. Drain the pasta using a spaghetti strainer to lift it out of the pot and into a bowl. Pour out the pasta water and place the spaghetti back in the pot you cooked it in. Add the green beans along with the oil they marinated in and cook for 3 minutes over medium heat while stirring. Transfer to a serving bowl and sprinkle with the grated pecorino cheese. Serve hot, with grated pecorino on the table.

Sedanini with Ricotta, Saffron, and Rosemary
Sedanini con Ricotta e Zafferano

Serves 6

"Sheep's-milk ricotta is always preferable to cow's-milk ricotta, if you can find it."

—G.

The saffron, orange, nutmeg, and rosemary together in this pasta are a gift of taste. We will never be able to thank our friend Kery enough for sharing this recipe with us. It is a great make-ahead dish. You can prepare the ricotta mixture up to a day ahead of time. Then, when you're ready to serve dinner, it only takes as much time as it takes to boil the pasta.

1. Bring a large saucepan of water to a boil. Stir in a small fistful of salt and the sedanini and boil until the pasta is tender. Reserve a cupful of the pasta water and drain the pasta quickly through a colander.

2. While the pasta is cooking, warm the milk and melt the saffron in it. Mix the ricotta, orange zest, beaten egg, saffron milk, nutmeg, salt, and pepper together in a mixing bowl.

3. Return the drained pasta to the pot you cooked it in. Add the ricotta *condimento* as well as the butter, oil, rosemary, and half the Parmesan. Add 1/2 cup of the reserved pasta water and toss the pasta with the *condimento* over medium heat for 2 minutes, just to warm, adding more pasta water until the pasta is slick, not sticky. Transfer the pasta to a pasta bowl. Sprinkle with the remaining Parmesan cheese and a few gratings of orange rind for color, and serve immediately, with grated Parmesan on the table.

Salt
1 pound sedanini
1/4 cup milk
Pinch of saffron threads or powder
3/4 pound fresh ricotta*
Zest of 1 orange, reserving some for
  grating over the pasta
1 egg, beaten
A few gratings of freshly grated
  nutmeg (or a pinch of ground
  nutmeg)
Freshly ground black pepper
6 tablespoons unsalted butter
1 tablespoon olive oil
1 tablespoon finely chopped fresh
  rosemary
2/3 cup (about 2 ounces) freshly
  grated Parmesan cheese, plus more
  to pass at the table

See source list.

The hillsides around Gangivecchio are filled with grazing sheep. To them, we give thanks for the tangy ricotta that is available to us, made fresh every day.

Tagliatelline with Zucchini Flowers and Fresh Herbs
Tagliatelline con Fiori di Zucca

Serves 6

This elegant dish is simple and quick to make. Don't forget: when you buy the zucchini flowers, choose those that are still almost closed. They are fresher and won't fall apart when you put them in the oil.

2/3 cup extra virgin olive oil, plus
  more for the pasta water
2 garlic cloves
1 *ciuffetto* (small bunch) fresh basil
  leaves, minced
1 *ciuffetto* (small bunch) fresh
  marjoram leaves, minced
2 pounds zucchini flowers, cleaned
Salt and freshly ground black pepper
1 pound tagliatellini
Freshly grated Parmesan cheese

1. Heat the oil in a saucepan over low heat. Add the garlic cloves and sauté for 2 minutes. Add the basil, marjoram, zucchini flowers, and salt and pepper to taste and continue to cook, stirring occasionally, until the flowers are soft, about 5 minutes.

2. While the flowers are cooking, bring a large saucepan of water to a boil. Stir in a small fistful of salt and a splash of olive oil. Stir in the tagliatellini and cook until al dente. Lift the pasta out of the water with a spaghetti strainer, reserving the pasta water. Put the pasta into the saucepan with the zucchini flowers. Add a splash of pasta water and heat the pasta with the *condimento* over high heat for 1 to 2 minutes, adding pasta water if it is sticky. Transfer the pasta to a serving bowl, sprinkle with Parmesan, and serve immediately. Pass the Parmesan.

"We never buy zucchini flowers; we only get them from our garden. Cleaning to us means to cut off the tough part of the stem and the stamens, and to make sure there are not bugs in the flowers."

—G.

Our word for a small bunch of herbs such as basil is the same as our word for the hair that falls over one's face: un ciuffo.

Classic Spaghetti with Tuna Roe
Classici Spaghetti alla Bottarga

Serves 6

Bottarga is pressed tuna roe. You find it in small bricks at Il Capo, the big market in Palermo, and it is worth its weight in gold. It comes from the island of Favignana, where our friend Maria Piera has a house on the sea. When we go in the summertime, we always have this classic spaghetti dish at least once a visit. In America, maybe you experiment with bottarga, *but to a Sicilian, there is only one thing to make with* bottarga, *and it is this.*

1. Heat the olive oil and the garlic cloves in a large frying pan over low heat until you smell a good garlic perfume—the garlic must not burn. Turn off the heat and transfer the hot oil with garlic to a serving bowl. Add the parsley, lemon zest, and grated *bottarga* and mix well.

2. Meanwhile, bring a large pot of water to a boil. Stir in a splash of olive oil and salt; don't use too much salt for this dish, as the *bottarga* is very salty. Add the spaghetti, stir, and boil until al dente.

3. Remove and discard the garlic cloves from the *condimento*. Lift the spaghetti out of the pot and into the bowl with the *condimento* using a spaghetti strainer. Don't worry if some water comes with the pasta; a little extra water will give the finished pasta a nice consistency. Mix the spaghetti with the *condimento*, and add more pasta water if it is sticky. Serve hot, with grated Parmesan cheese.

3/4 cup extra virgin olive oil, plus
   more for the pasta water
3 garlic cloves
2 tablespoons finely chopped fresh
   Italian parsley
Grated zest of 1 lemon
2 tablespoons finely grated *bottarga*
1 pound spaghetti
Freshly grated Parmesan cheese

INSALATA SICILIANA
My friend Claire recently brought us a gift of a large brick of **bottarga**, so I experimented and created this salad out of all very Sicilian ingredients. For **4** people, slice **4** fennel bulbs crosswise very thin. Peel and slice **2** big blood oranges. Mix the fennel and orange slices in a big bowl with enough extra virgin olive oil to coat, a squeeze of lemon juice, and freshly ground black pepper. Transfer the vegetables to a serving platter, pour the oil mixture over them, and top with three very thin slices of **bottarga**.

Agrigento–Style Garlic and Oil Spaghetti with Saffron
Spaghetti Aglio e Olio di Agrigento

Serves 6

This pasta is something good that came out of a very painful event: going to the dentist. My dentist is in the town of Agrigento. Once when I visited, I was so tired afterward that I ate in the albergo *where I stayed. The chef said that to resuscitate me, he would prepare this pasta for me. It was so good that I must say for a moment I forgot my pain. They usually make it with spaghetti, but that night, he made it with a pasta called* lingua di passera, *which means "tongue of the singing birds." It's something we usually cook only for babies, but they gave it to me to comfort me. —G.*

Salt
1 pound spaghetti
1/3 cup extra virgin olive oil, plus
   more for the pasta water
8 tablespoons (1 stick) unsalted butter
3 garlic cloves
Pinch of saffron threads or powder
1 large fresh tomato, peeled, seeded,
   and chopped
Pinch of cayenne pepper
1/3 cup minced fresh Italian parsley
Freshly grated Parmesan cheese

1. Bring a large saucepan of water to a boil. Stir in a small fistful of salt and a splash of olive oil. Stir in the spaghetti and boil, stirring often, until it is al dente.

2. While the pasta is cooking, warm the oil and butter together in a large frying pan over low heat until the butter is melted. Add the garlic and cook until it is fragrant and light golden, about 5 minutes.

3. Ladle out half a cup of hot pasta water. Melt the saffron in the hot water and add to the garlic oil.

4. Use a spaghetti strainer to lift the spaghetti out of the pasta water and into the frying pan with the butter and oil. Don't worry if you bring water with the spaghetti; the water will help make the pasta smooth and moist. Add the chopped tomato, cayenne pepper, and parsley and mix well. Cook the spaghetti with the *condimento* for 2 to 3 minutes just to warm the tomatoes. Transfer the pasta to a serving dish, dust with grated Parmesan cheese, and serve immediately with more grated Parmesan on the table.

"I think Italians have more words for flavors than anyone else, like Eskimos have more words for snow."   **—W.**

Mezze Maniche with Sun-Dried Tomatoes and Green Olives
Mezze Maniche con Pomodori Secchi

Serves 4

This recipe came from my friend Catarina, who lives in western Sicily, where outside every house you see the bright red color of tomatoes being dried. Women lay the fresh tomatoes, cut in half, on long wooden tables to let them dry in the sun.

1. Mince the garlic and parsley together and place them in a bowl. Add the sun-dried tomatoes, olives, and anchovy paste and mix well.

2. Bring a large saucepan of water to a boil. Stir in a small fistful of salt and the pasta and boil until the pasta is tender.

3. While the pasta is cooking, heat the olive oil in a large frying pan over medium-high heat. Add the tomato-olive mixture and sauté for 1 minute. Add 3/4 cup of hot pasta water, adjust the salt and pepper to taste (be careful because the anchovy paste is salty), and simmer for 5 minutes.

4. Reserve a cupful of the pasta water and drain in a colander. Quickly transfer the pasta to the frying pan with sauce and sauté over high heat for 2 to 3 minutes, for the pasta to absorb the sauce. Transfer to a serving bowl, dust with Parmesan cheese, and serve immediately, with more Parmesan passed at the table.

1 garlic clove
2 tablespoons fresh Italian parsley
4 sun-dried tomatoes in olive oil, cut into thin strips
10 pitted green olives, sliced into rounds
1 tablespoon anchovy paste
Salt
1 pound mezze maniche
1/2 cup extra virgin olive oil
Freshly ground black pepper
Freshly grated Parmesan cheese

MEZZE MANICHE
means "short sleeves." They are in fact little rectangular sheets of pasta. It is the great fantasy of our pasta makers that the shape resembles a short shirtsleeve. Any small pasta shape, such as farfalle, will also work with this recipe.

Large green olives are often known outside Sicily as Sicilian olives, though in fact we grow many varieties.

Tagliolini with Green Apple Pesto and Speck
Tagliolini con Mela Verdi e Speck

Serves 6

2 Granny Smith apples, cored and cut into cubes
2 cups loosely packed mixed baby lettuce
2 tablespoons pine nuts
1 garlic clove
2 tablespoons lemon juice
1/2 cup extra virgin olive oil, plus more for the pasta water
Salt and freshly ground black pepper
2 tablespoons butter, cut into small pieces
1 pound fresh or dried egg tagliolini (see Fresh Pasta Dough, page 8)
1/2 pound speck, cut into cubes

TAGLIOLINI

is a fresh pasta, made with eggs and shaped like a thin tagliatelle. The name means "cut" because they are cut with scissors from the sheet of fresh pasta. We used to have to make these at home if we wanted them, but today we can find them in every food shop. This shape is often cooked in broth.

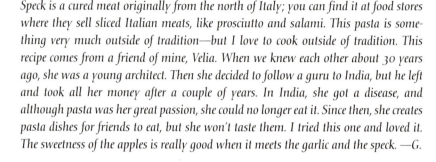

Speck is a cured meat originally from the north of Italy; you can find it at food stores where they sell sliced Italian meats, like prosciutto and salami. This pasta is something very much outside of tradition—but I love to cook outside of tradition. This recipe comes from a friend of mine, Velia. When we knew each other about 30 years ago, she was a young architect. Then she decided to follow a guru to India, but he left and took all her money after a couple of years. In India, she got a disease, and although pasta was her great passion, she could no longer eat it. Since then, she creates pasta dishes for friends to eat, but she won't taste them. I tried this one and loved it. The sweetness of the apples is really good when it meets the garlic and the speck. —G.

1. Put the apples in the bowl of a food processor fitted with a metal blade, add the baby lettuce, pine nuts, garlic, lemon juice, olive oil, and salt and pepper to taste, and puree. Add some oil if necessary to obtain a creamy, spreadable paste. Transfer to a serving bowl and add the butter pieces.
2. Bring a large saucepan of water to a boil. Stir in a small fistful of salt and a splash of olive oil. Stir in the tagliolini and cook, stirring often, until the pasta is al dente.
3. Meanwhile, add 1/4 cup of the boiling pasta water to the bowl with the *condimento*. Reserve a cupful of the pasta water and drain the pasta quickly in a colander. Transfer it to the pasta bowl. Add the cubed speck and mix very well, adding hot pasta water if it is dry or sticky. Serve immediately.

Cavatelli with Arugula and Pecorino
Cavatelli con Rucola e Pecorino

Serves 6

Arugula and pecorino make a wonderful combination, and one that is very much of our countryside. Our friend Vincenzo, who lived in the country, was always inventing new dishes with this combination. This pasta is a tribute to him.

1. Heat 2 tablespoons of the olive oil with 2 tablespoons of water in a frying pan over medium-high heat. Add the sliced onions and the red pepper, and sauté for about 10 minutes, until the onions are tender and golden brown. Add the tomato sauce and simmer for 10 minutes. Add the basil leaves and adjust for salt to taste. Remove and discard the pepper.

2. Bring a large saucepan of water to a boil. Stir in a small fistful of salt and the pasta and cook the pasta until tender. Reserve a cupful of the pasta water and drain the pasta in a colander.

3. Quickly transfer the pasta to a serving bowl. Add the arugula and the tomato sauce, grated pecorino, remaining 2 tablespoons of olive oil, and hot pasta water, if necessary, and toss so that the arugula wilts. Sprinkle with pecorino and serve immediately, with more grated pecorino on the table.

1/4 cup extra virgin olive oil
1 medium white or yellow onion, sliced
1 small whole hot red pepper
2 cups Fresh Tomato Sauce (page 9; or bottled sauce*)
6 to 8 fresh basil leaves
Salt
1 pound cavatelli
1/2 pound fresh arugula, washed, dried, and torn with your hands
1 cup (about 3 ounces) freshly grated pecorino cheese, plus more for passing at the table

See source list.

Spaghetti Carbonara
Spaghetti alla Carbonara

Serves 4

This is not a Sicilian dish, but it is a dish we like very much. It's important that the eggs you use for this are very fresh because they are added at the last minute and are virtually uncooked.

Salt
1/3 cup extra virgin olive oil, plus
   more for the pasta water
1 pound spaghetti
5 large egg yolks
1/3 cup (about 1 ounce) freshly grated
   pecorino cheese
Freshly ground black pepper
4 tablespoons (1/2 stick) unsalted
   butter
1/4 pound pancetta (or bacon), cut
   into 1/2-inch cubes
Freshly grated Parmesan cheese

"One of the most awful things I ever saw was in England: canned spaghetti."

—G.

1. Bring a large saucepan of water to a boil. Stir in a small fistful of salt and a splash of olive oil. Add the spaghetti and cook, stirring often so it doesn't stick together, until the pasta is al dente.

2. While the pasta is cooking, whisk the egg yolks in a serving bowl with the pecorino cheese and some black pepper. Add 3 tablespoons of hot pasta water to the eggs and whisk again.

3. Warm the olive oil and butter in a large frying pan over medium heat until the butter is melted. Add the pancetta and sauté for about 3 minutes, until it is golden brown.

4. Remove the pasta from the water using a spaghetti strainer and transfer it to the serving bowl with the eggs and cheese. Toss very quickly, adding some pasta water if the *condimento* is too thick or dry. Add the cooked pancetta and toss again. Sprinkle with freshly grated Parmesan cheese and serve immediately with more Parmesan and a pepper grinder on the table.

Pink Spaghetti with Anchovies and Breadcrumbs
Spaghetti con Acciughe e Mollica Rossa

Serves 6

This is a very old Sicilian recipe. The ingredients are very inexpensive. It is a poor dish, but it is something you like even if you are not poor—or maybe especially if you are not! When you go to any not-very-fancy restaurant in Sicily, you can ask for spaghetti with anchovies and the waiter will be sure to ask you, "Red or white?" Everyone knows what he means: With tomato sauce or without tomato sauce? We prefer it with tomato sauce.

1. Heat the olive oil with the anchovies and tomato paste in a large saucepan over medium heat. Simmer the ingredients together for about 10 minutes, until the anchovies have dissolved. Season with salt and pepper to taste. (You may not need any salt because of the saltiness of the anchovies.)

2. Meanwhile, bring a big saucepan of water to a boil over high heat. Stir in a small fistful of salt to taste and a splash of olive oil. Add the spaghetti and stir to prevent the strands from sticking together. Boil until the spaghetti is al dente, stirring often.

3. When the spaghetti is almost done, put the *condimento* into a serving bowl. Lift the spaghetti out of the water with a spaghetti strainer and straight into the bowl with the *condimento*. Toss the pasta, adding a little pasta water if the pasta is dry or sticky. Top with a sprinkling of the toasted breadcrumbs. Serve immediately, passing toasted breadcrumbs at the table as you would grated cheese.

1/2 cup extra virgin olive oil, plus
   more for the pasta water
12 anchovy fillets in oil
2 cups tomato paste
Salt and freshly ground black pepper
1 pound spaghetti
Toasted breadcrumbs

Linguine with Scallions, Raisins, and Turmeric
Linguine con lo Scalogno e Curcuma

Serves 6

Turmeric is one of the many ingredients that came to us from Tunisia. We like it both for the color and the flavor and think of it as the poor people's saffron.

8 tablespoons (1 stick) unsalted butter
6 scallions, thinly sliced (white part only)
1/2 cup raisins, soaked in tepid water for 10 minutes
1/4 cup heavy cream
1 tablespoon turmeric
Salt and freshly ground black pepper
Olive oil for the pasta water
1 pound linguine
Freshly grated Parmesan cheese

TIP Butter will never burn if you add a little water to it.

1. Melt the butter with 2 tablespoons of water in a large frying pan on very low heat; be careful not to let it brown. Add the scallions and sauté, stirring often, for 5 minutes or until the scallions are golden. Drain the soaked raisins, add them to the frying pan with the scallions, and sauté another 2 minutes. Stir in the cream, turmeric, a few tablespoons of hot water, and salt and pepper to taste. Mix well and cook for about 3 minutes to bring the flavors together.
2. Meanwhile, bring a large saucepan of water to a boil. Stir in a small fistful of salt and a splash of olive oil. Add the linguine and cook, stirring often, until the pasta is al dente. Lift the linguine out of the water with a spaghetti strainer and put it directly into the frying pan with the scallions. Toss the pasta with the *condimento* on high heat for 1 or 2 minutes to warm through. Transfer the pasta to a serving bowl, sprinkle with Parmesan cheese, and serve immediately, with Parmesan on the table.

Tagliatelle with Fresh Tomato and Garlic
Tagliatelle con Salsa Picchio Pacchio

Serves 6

Don't ask what picchio pacchio *means. It just means* picchio pacchio, *which is a* condimento *of fresh peeled tomato, a little garlic, and fresh parsley. If you like herbs, add a handful of fresh chopped basil or dried oregano to this.*

1. Heat the olive oil with the garlic in a large frying pan over medium heat and cook for 5 minutes, until the garlic is very aromatic—but be careful not to let it brown. Stir in the tomatoes, sugar, and salt and pepper to taste and sauté over medium heat for about 10 minutes, to soften the tomatoes. Taste the sauce and add more salt, pepper, or sugar to taste.

2. Meanwhile, bring a large saucepan of water to a boil. Stir in a small fistful of salt and a splash of olive oil. Add the tagliatelle and stir to keep it from sticking together. Cook until the pasta is al dente.

3. While the pasta is cooking, spoon half of the *condimento* into a serving bowl. Lift the pasta out of the water with a spaghetti strainer and into the serving bowl with the *condimento*. When you have half the pasta in the bowl, add a splash of hot pasta water and toss. Add the remaining pasta and the remaining *condimento* and more pasta water if the pasta is sticky, and toss again. Sprinkle with Parmesan cheese and serve immediately, with more Parmesan at the table.

1/2 cup extra virgin olive oil, plus
   more for the pasta water
2 garlic cloves
2 1/4 pounds fresh tomatoes, peeled,
   seeded, and chopped
1 tablespoon sugar (or more to taste)
Salt and freshly ground black pepper
1 pound tagliatelle
Freshly grated Parmesan cheese

Quick Tagliatelle with Fried Zucchini and Parsley
Pasta Veloce con Zucchine e Prezzemolo

Serves 6

In Italian, we have a saying: "Sei come il prezzemolo. Dovunque!" This means, "You are like parsley. Everywhere!" This is a beautiful pasta to make with your summertime zucchini—quick and full of flavor.

Extra virgin olive oil for frying the
  zucchini and for the pasta water
2 pounds zucchini, sliced 3/4 inch
  thick
Salt
1 pound tagliatelle
1/2 cup finely chopped fresh
  Italian parsley
Freshly grated Parmesan cheese

"When we say olive oil, we always mean 'extra virgin.' It is the only kind of olive oil we have on the property at Gangivecchio."

—G.

1. Heat enough olive oil in a large frying pan to fill it to 1 inch. Add the zucchini slices in 1 layer so they aren't touching each other and fry, turning only once, until they are golden brown on both sides. Remove with a slotted spoon and place them in a bowl. (Do not drain on paper towels; the oil from frying will be your *condimento*.) Repeat with the remaining zucchini. Season with salt.

2. Bring a big saucepan of water to a boil. Stir in a small fistful of salt and a splash of oil. Stir in the tagliatelle and boil, stirring often, until the pasta is al dente.

3. Meanwhile, place one-quarter of the zucchini in the bottom of a serving bowl. Sprinkle with 1/8 cup of the parsley. Add a ladleful of pasta water. When the pasta is done, lift it out of the water and into the bowl with the zucchini in layers, adding some zucchini and some minced parsley as you go and adding all the zucchini oil. Toss very well, adding more pasta water until the pasta is slippery. Sprinkle with grated Parmesan cheese and pass more Parmesan at the table.

OPPOSITE: *The altar is in Palermo Vecchio, or Centro Storico (Historical Center), where old Sicilian is still spoken in the streets.*

Rich Pastas
(Pastasciutta Ricca)

25. Giovanna's Lasagnette with Creamy Tomato Sauce, Toasted Almonds, and Pecorino Cheese (*Lasagnette Rosa di Giovanna*)

26. Spaghetti with Eggplant, Swordfish, and Mint (*Pasta Trinacria*)

27. Bavette with Pistachio Pesto and Shrimp (*Pesto di Pistacchi con Gamberi*)

28. Paolo's Arugula Pesto the Chez Panisse Way (*Il Pesto di Rucola di Paolo Stile Chez Panisse*)

29. Casareccia with Gangivecchio's Five-Nut Pesto (*Casareccia con Pesto di Frutta Secca di Gangivecchio*)

30. Fusilli with Porcini Mushrooms, Aromatic Vegetables, and Grappa Cream Sauce (*La Pasta Profumata con Funghi Porcini e Grappa*)

31. Lumache Rigate with Broccoli Flowers and Turmeric Cream (*Lumache Rigate con Cimette di Broccoli e Crema di Curcuma*)

32. Farfalle with Pancetta, Chickpeas, and Saffron (*Farfalle con Ceci e Pancetta*)

33. Maria's Sedanini with Salmon, Fennel, and Rosemary (*Sedanini al Profumo di Mare di Maria*)

34. Sedanini Rigate with Summer Vegetable Puree (*Sedanini Rigate con Crema di Verdure*)

35. Festonate with Gorgonzola, Mascarpone, and Walnuts (*Festonate con Gorgonzola, Mascarpone e Noci*)

36. La Cambusa's Linguine with Shrimp, Zucchini, and Cherry Tomatoes (*Le Linguine con Gamberi, Zucchine e Pomodorini della Cambusa*)

37. Paolo's Pennette with Fresh Figs and Pancetta (*Pennette con Fichi e Pancetta di Paolo*)

38. Bucato with a Carnival of Sweet Peppers (*Bucato con Carnevale di Peperoni Dolci*)

39. Shells with Fresh Fava Beans and Ricotta (*Conchiglie con Fave Fresche e Ricotta*)

40. Ditalini with Creamed Winter Squash and Nutmeg (*Ditalini con Crema di Zucca Rossa d'Inverno*)

41. Tagliatelline with Pancetta, Mint, and a Rainbow of Summer Vegetables (*Arcobaleno di Tagliatelline*)

42. Casareccia with Zucchini and Its Flowers (*Casareccia con Fiori di Zucca*)

43. Farfalle with Springtime Vegetables and Pecorino Cheese (*Farfalle Primavera*)

44. "Straw and Hay" with Green Peas and Lettuce in Prosciutto Cream Sauce (*Paglia e Fieno con Piselli e Lattuga*)

45. Rigatoni with Swordfish Ragù (*Rigatoni con Ragù di Pesce Spada*)

46. Ditalini Cooked like Risotto with Wild Mushrooms (*Ditalini Come Risotto*)

47. Pappardelle with Asparagus, Walnuts, and Speck (*Pappardelle con Asparagi, Noci e Speck*)

48. Rigatoni with Fried Eggplant, Wild Fennel, and Fresh Sardines (*Rigatoni con Melanzane Fritte, Finocchietti e Sarde*)

49. Fusilli with Sausages and Potato (*Fusilli con Salsiccia e Patate*)

50. Sicily's Famous Spaghetti with Eggplant and Ricotta Salata (*Spaghetti alla Norma*)

51. Paolo's Pappardelle with Lamb and Fava Beans Braised in Red Wine (*Pappardelle con Fave ed Agnello di Paolo*)

52. Pasta with Lentil Ragù
   (*Pasta con Ragù di Lenticchie*)

53. Bucatini with Sausages, Pecorino, and Cinnamon
   (*Bucatini con Salsiccia e Pecorino alla Madonita*)

54. Little Penne with Potatoes and Eggs
   (*Pennette con Patate e Uova*)

55. Tubetti with Salt Cod and Broccoli Rabe
   (*Tubetti con Baccalà e Cime di Rapa*)

56. Spaghetti with Clams and Mushrooms
   (*Spaghetti con Vongole e Funghi*)

57. Fusilli with Fresh Shell Beans
   (*Fusilli con Fagioli Freschi*)

58. Bucatini with Dried Figs
   (*Bucatini con Fichi Secchi*)

59. Farfalle with Artichoke Hearts, Fava Beans, and Peas
   (*Farfalle con Carciofi, Fave e Piselli*)

60. Tagliatelle with Meat Gravy and Porcini Mushrooms
   (*Tagliatelle con Sugo di Arrosto e Porcini*)

61. Ditali with Cauliflower and Cinnamon
   (*Ditali con Broccoli e Cannella*)

62. Bucatini with Sardines, Fennel, Pine Nuts, and Currants
   (*Bucatini con le Sarde*)

63. Bucatini with Cauliflower, Currants, and Pine Nuts
   (*Bucatini alla Palina*)

64. Orietta's Linguine with Shrimp and Fried Artichokes
   (*Linguine con Gamberi e Carciofi Fritti di Orietta*)

65. Lasagne Ricce with Fresh Sausages
   (*Lasagne Ricce con Ragù di Salsiccia*)

When we went to America on promotional tours for our first books, we were surprised at how rich the pasta was. No wonder you think it is unhealthy to eat pasta every day! In fact, we usually eat very simple pastas. While the pasta recipes in this chapter are the most flavorful, if eaten at lunch they usually call for a short nap afterward—and just a light meal at the end of the day.

means "little lasagnes," which is what these are–thin flat pasta. If you do not have lasagnette, you can use fettuccine or pappardelle, another thin flat pasta, in its place.

Giovanna's Lasagnette with Creamy Tomato Sauce, Toasted Almonds, and Pecorino Cheese
Lasagnette Rosa di Giovanna

Serves 6

Almonds are very popular in the cooking of western Sicily. We happen to love them. In this dish, we call for egg pasta. We use egg pasta when we are in the mood for it—otherwise it is always semolina pasta. The difference is that egg pasta is a little fancier than semolina pasta and tastes richer. It's also more expensive.

One 16-ounce can peeled whole
   tomatoes, drained in a colander
   and broken into pieces with
   your hands
2 garlic cloves
1 cup whole fresh basil leaves
1/2 cup fresh Italian parsley leaves
1/2 cup extra virgin olive oil, plus
   more for the pasta water
1/2 cup grated pecorino cheese
2 large egg yolks
2 cups shelled almonds,
   coarsely chopped
1 teaspoon salt, plus more for
   the pasta water
1/2 teaspoon freshly ground
   black pepper
1 pound egg lasagnette
Freshly grated Parmesan cheese

1. Put the tomatoes in a large frying pan and sauté them over medium heat for about 5 minutes or until they begin to break down and give off juices. Pass the cooked tomatoes through a food mill into a big bowl.

2. Put the garlic cloves, basil and parsley leaves, oil, pecorino cheese, egg yolks, half of the almonds, salt, and pepper in the bowl of a food processor fitted with a metal blade and puree until you have a paste with a grainy texture.

3. Meanwhile, bring a large saucepan of water to a boil. Stir in a splash of olive oil, salt, and the lasagnette and cook, stirring often, until the pasta is al dente. Reserve some of the pasta water and drain the pasta quickly in a colander.

4. While the pasta is cooking, put the remaining almonds in a dry skillet and toast them over medium heat, shaking the pan very often–otherwise they burn instantly–until golden brown and fragrant.

5. Put the pasta back in the same pot you cooked it in, over high heat. Add the paste, the tomatoes, and 1/4 cup of reserved pasta water. Toss it all together for 1 to 2 minutes, adding more pasta water if the pasta is dry or sticky. Transfer to a large serving dish. Top with the chopped almonds and sprinkle with Parmesan cheese. Serve immediately. Pass the Parmesan at the table.

Spaghetti with Eggplant, Swordfish, and Mint
Pasta Trinacria

Serves 6

The national symbol of Sicily is a drawing of a human head with no body, just three legs extending directly from the head. It is called the Trinacria, which means "triangular," referring to the shape of Sicily. The three legs represent the three capes of the island. We named this pasta Trinacria because eggplant, swordfish, and mint are three fundamental ingredients of the Sicilian kitchen.

1. Heat the olive oil with the garlic in a saucepan over medium heat, stirring often and making sure the garlic doesn't burn, just lightly browns. Break the tomatoes apart into the frying pan with your hands. Pour any remaining juices from the canned tomatoes into the frying pan. Season with salt and pepper and simmer over medium heat for 10 minutes, or until the juices reduce and thicken. Stir in the swordfish and chopped mint and simmer for about 10 minutes, or until the swordfish is cooked through. Turn off the heat.

2. While the sauce is simmering, pour the oil into a large frying pan to fill to 2 1/2–3 inches deep. Heat the oil over medium–high heat until it is very hot but not smoking. Carefully place the eggplant cubes in the oil and fry, turning them until they are golden brown on all sides. Remove the eggplant from the oil using a slotted spoon and drain on a bed of paper towels. A few minutes before tossing the sauce with the pasta, stir in the eggplant.

3. Meanwhile, bring a large saucepan of water to a boil. Stir in a small fistful of salt and a splash of olive oil. Add the spaghetti and stir. Cook, stirring often so that the strands don't stick together, until the spaghetti is al dente. Lift the spaghetti out of the pasta water and into the frying pan with the tomato sauce placed over high heat. Toss the pasta with the sauce for about 2 minutes, adding hot pasta water to the pan if the pasta is sticky. Transfer the spaghetti to a serving bowl and serve immediately, topped with fresh mint leaves.

1/2 cup extra virgin olive oil, plus more for the pasta water

3 garlic cloves, slivered

One 28–ounce can peeled whole tomatoes

Salt and freshly ground black pepper

1 pound swordfish steak, skinned and cut into 1/2–inch cubes

1/4 cup chopped fresh mint, plus whole mint leaves for garnishing the pasta

Safflower or other vegetable oil for deep-frying

2 medium eggplant, cut into 1–inch cubes

1 pound spaghetti

Bavette with Pistachio Pesto and Shrimp
Pesto di Pistacchi con Gamberi

Serves 4

BAVETTE

There is no translation for this long pasta. It is a close relative of tagliatelle and linguine, thinner than the first, thicker than the second. Either can be substituted.

3 garlic cloves
2 cups whole basil leaves
1 cup shelled pistachios
1/4 cup pine nuts
1 cup extra virgin olive oil
1 teaspoon salt, plus more
  for the pasta water
4 tablespoons (1/2 stick) unsalted
  butter
1/2 pound small shrimp,
  peeled and boiled
3/4 pound bavette
3/4 pound almonds, lightly
  toasted and chopped
Freshly grated Parmesan cheese

I had this in a restaurant in Selinunte, a small seaside town in western Sicily famous for its enormous Greek temples. I love to visit historic places, but afterward I am always exhausted and the only cure is a big bowl of pasta. —G.

TIP We don't blend pesto completely into a paste because we like to taste the nuts and the basil under our teeth.

1. Put the garlic cloves, basil leaves, pistachios, pine nuts, 1/4 cup of the olive oil, and salt into the bowl of a food processor fitted with a metal blade and blend. Gradually pour the rest of the oil through the feed tube until all the ingredients are integrated into a paste with a slightly coarse texture. The pesto must be fluid, not hard or dry. If it is not fluid, turn the food processor back on and add more oil until you have a runny paste.

2. Put the pesto in a large serving bowl, reserving a large spoonful. Place the butter and the cooked shrimp on top of the pesto.

3. Bring a large saucepan of water to a boil. Stir in a small fistful of salt, a splash of olive oil, and the bavette and cook, stirring often so the pasta doesn't stick together, until the pasta is al dente.

4. While the pasta is cooking, toast the almonds in a dry skillet over medium heat, shaking the pan constantly so the almonds don't burn.

5. Lift the pasta out of the pot and into the bowl with the pesto, butter, and shrimp. Add a splash of pasta water and toss the pasta until the butter is melted and the pasta is coated. Add the toasted almonds and toss again. *A tavola!* Dust with Parmesan cheese and serve very hot, with more Parmesan on the table.

TIP We don't taste pesto when we make it, because pesto gives its best flavor when it is hot, with pasta.

Bavette with Pistachio Pesto and Shrimp

Paolo's Arugula Pesto the Chez Panisse Way
Il Pesto di Rucola di Paolo Stile Chez Panisse

Serves 6

4 cups loosely packed arugula leaves, washed and dried well

2 garlic cloves, crushed in a mortar with a pinch of salt

1/2 cup walnuts, lightly toasted, skins rubbed off, and pounded in a mortar to a paste

1/2 cup pine nuts, lightly toasted, pounded in a mortar to a paste

1/3 cup freshly grated pecorino cheese

1/3 cup freshly grated Parmesan cheese

1/2 cup extra virgin olive oil, more if needed, plus more for the pasta water

Salt and freshly ground black pepper

1 pound spaghetti

1 tablespoon unsalted butter

TIP Adding butter to any pasta when you toss it gives it a creamier texture and brings out the flavor of the *condimento*.

Many years ago, when we were touring for our first book, Alice Waters invited us to cook a dinner at her famous, very special restaurant, Chez Panisse, in California. After that dinner, of course we gave the chefs at the restaurant a copy of the book. From that, they learned to make Paolo's arugula pesto, and have continued to make it in the winter, when basil is not in season, ever since. Here, the chefs have been kind enough to share their secrets for making our pasta.

We add pine nuts for sweetness, as walnuts can sometimes add to the rocket's (another word for arugula) inherent bitterness. For the same reason, we rub the skins off the toasted walnuts. We also use both pecorino and Parmesan cheeses as the arugula pesto seems to want more cheese than basil pesto would. And lastly, rather than adding pureed tomatoes, we toss in sun-dried tomato pieces, sparingly, with the pasta at the end. Also, a note: we always use a blender for pesto making, not a food processor. And we are sure to not let it run any longer than necessary—it should always be grinding new leaves, not just regrinding what is already done. To that end, we like to pack the blender with ingredients, pulse, push down, pulse, stir, pulse, stir, and add a little more oil if needed as we go. Stop blending when it is just pureed. A slightly chunky pesto is much preferable to an overpureed one.

1. Put the arugula, garlic, walnuts, pine nuts, pecorino, and Parmesan in the jar of a blender and pulse to coarsely chop. Pack it down, add the oil, and pulse again. Continue to pulse, opening up the blender to stir the ingredients so the blade is always cutting new leaves, until the pesto is almost pureed to a paste but is not smooth. Add more oil if necessary to form a loose paste and adjust the salt and pepper to taste. Transfer the pesto to the bottom of a pasta bowl.

2. Bring a large saucepan of water to a boil. Stir in a small fistful of salt, a splash of olive oil, and the spaghetti and boil until the spaghetti is al dente. Lift the spaghetti out of the pot and into the bowl with the pesto. Add the butter and a splash of pasta water and toss to coat, adding more pasta water until the spaghetti is slippery. Sprinkle with a dusting of Parmesan and serve immediately, with Parmesan at the table.

Casareccia with Gangivecchio's Five–Nut Pesto
Casareccia con Pesto di Frutta Secca di Gangivecchio

Serves 12

Five-nut pesto is one of the victories of our gardens and our kitchen. All the nuts but the pistachios come from our own trees. We don't have pistachios because you need to have both the male and female trees to produce nuts, and our females died. Still, we buy only the best Sicilian pistachios, from the town of Bronte.

1. Put the almonds, hazelnuts, walnuts, pistachios, pine nuts, garlic, basil, parsley, Parmesan, pecorino, and salt and pepper to taste in a food processor fitted with a metal blade. Turn on the machine and immedi–ately begin pouring the olive oil in a thin stream through the feed tube. Continue to puree and add the oil until the ingredients have formed a paste with a spreadable consistency. Do not overpuree; the nuts should retain some of their texture. Adjust the salt and pepper to taste, running the machine just to mix in the seasoning. Scrape the pesto into a saucepan.

2. Bring a separate, large saucepan of water to a boil over high heat. Stir in a small fistful of salt and the casareccia and cook until the pasta is tender.

3. While the pasta is cooking, stir 2 cups of the boiling pasta water and the butter into the saucepan with the pesto and place over low heat to warm through.

4. Reserve a cupful of the pasta water and drain the pasta quickly in a colander. Quickly transfer the pasta to a serving bowl along with 1 cup of the pesto. Toss and continue adding the pesto, a cup at a time, along with a splash of the reserved pasta water if the pasta is sticky or dry, until the pasta is coated. Serve immediately, with Parmesan on the table.

1/2 cup almonds
1/2 cup hazelnuts
1/2 cup walnuts
1/2 cup pistachios
1/2 cup pine nuts
6 garlic cloves
2 cups fresh basil leaves, plus more
  for garnish, washed and dried well
1/3 cup chopped fresh Italian parsley
1/2 cup freshly grated Parmesan
  cheese, plus more for passing
  at the table
1/2 cup freshly grated pecorino
  cheese
Salt and freshly ground black pepper
3/4 cup extra virgin olive oil, or more
  as needed
2 pounds casareccia (gemelli) or
  penne
2 tablespoons unsalted butter

Sicily is famous for having the best pistachios in the world. They come from a town called Bronte in the eastern part of the island near Catania.

Fusilli with Porcini Mushrooms, Aromatic Vegetables, and Grappa Cream Sauce
La Pasta Profumata con Funghi Porcini e Grappa

Serves 6

We like the flavor of grappa in a simple pasta dish like this, because it's drier and has a subtler flavor than Marsala, Sicily's most famous cooking wine.

1 carrot, coarsely chopped
2 stalks celery, coarsely chopped
1 small white or yellow onion, coarsely chopped
1 garlic clove
2 tablespoons unsalted butter
1/4 cup extra virgin olive oil
3 tablespoons finely chopped fresh Italian parsley
1/2 cup dried porcini mushrooms, soaked in hot water for 20 minutes and minced
1/4 cup grappa
1 1/2 cups veal or beef broth
Salt and freshly ground black pepper
1/2 teaspoon cayenne pepper or hot pepper flakes
2/3 cup heavy cream
1 pound fusilli corti
1/2 cup freshly grated Parmesan cheese, plus more for passing at the table

TIP If oil and butter are smoking in the pan, it's too hot to sauté vegetables. They will burn immediately. Take the pan off the fire and let it cool until it stops smoking.

1. Put the carrots, celery, onions, and garlic into the bowl of a food processor fitted with a metal blade. Run the processor until the vegetables are minced but not pureed, or mince by hand.

2. Heat the butter and oil in a large saucepan over medium heat. Add the minced vegetables, 2 tablespoons of the parsley, and the minced porcini mushrooms to the pan and sauté for 2 to 3 minutes, until they begin to soften. Pour the grappa over the vegetables and cook for about 1 minute to evaporate the alcohol. Add the veal broth and sauté for 15 to 20 minutes, until the vegetables are very mushy, almost like a paste. Add more hot water (or broth) if the vegetables are sticking to the pan. Season with salt, pepper, and hot pepper. Stir in the cream and cook for 1 minute, just to warm the cream. If you cook it any longer, the cream will separate. Take the pan off the heat.

3. Meanwhile, bring a large saucepan of water to a boil. Stir in a small fistful of salt and the fusilli corti and cook until the pasta is tender. Reserve a cupful of the water and quickly drain the pasta in a colander.

4. Return the *condimento* to high heat. Add the drained pasta and about 1/2 cup of pasta water to the pan and stir to coat the pasta evenly with the *condimento*. Add the Parmesan cheese, and more pasta water if the pasta is sticky, and stir again. Transfer to a pasta bowl and sprinkle with the remaining minced parsley. Serve very hot with Parmesan at the table.

TIP When we think the *condimento* might be over–salty, we don't salt the pasta water. Then, just before the pasta is done, we taste a piece with the *condimento*. If it needs more salt, we add it to the water then. But we never, ever add salt to the pasta itself. The idea is to get the salt *in* the pasta, not sitting on top of it.

Lumache Rigate with Broccoli Flowers and Turmeric Cream
Lumache Rigate con Cimette di Broccoli e Crema di Curcuma

Serves 6

Turmeric is something I discovered from a girlfriend of my brother's. She was very fond of Tunisian flavors. I loved the color so much I found many different ways to use it. Turmeric gives a nice yellow color to a dish without adding as much flavor as saffron or curry. —G.

1. Bring a big pot of unsalted water to a boil. Cut the broccoli into florets. Discard the stems. Put the broccoli florets into the boiling water and cook them until they are tender and beginning to fall apart. Lift the broccoli out of the water with a strainer or slotted spoon; reserve the water to cook the pasta in.

2. Toast the pine nuts in a dry skillet over medium heat until they are golden brown. Move the pan around occasionally so the nuts cook on all sides and don't burn.

3. Bring the water you cooked the broccoli in back to a boil. Stir in a small fistful of salt. Add the lumache, stirring from time to time, and cook until it is tender.

4. While the pasta is cooking, heat the garlic and olive oil in a large frying pan over low heat until the garlic begins to give off a nice aroma. Add the drained broccoli and turn the heat up to medium. Add salt and pepper to taste and sauté the broccoli, using a wooden spoon to break up any big pieces, adding more water to the pan if the broccoli is sticking. Stir in the cream and the turmeric. Add a splash of hot pasta water if the *condimento* is too thick.

5. Drain the pasta in a colander and add it to the frying pan with the *condimento.* Sauté the pasta with the *condimento* until the pasta is coated. Sprinkle with Parmesan cheese and the toasted pine nuts. Serve immediately, with more Parmesan at the table.

TIP We never put salt in the water when boiling green vegetables. We think they stay greener if the water is not salted.

TIP Before you taste this snail-shaped pasta, lift one piece up with a fork and make sure to drain all the water from inside. I learned this the hard way the first time I cooked lumache—by burning my mouth, of course. —G.

2 medium heads broccoli
1/4 cup pine nuts
Salt
1 pound lumache rigate
4 cloves garlic
3 tablespoons extra virgin olive oil
Freshly ground black pepper
1 teaspoon turmeric
1/4 cup heavy cream
Freshly grated Parmesan cheese

LUMACHE
means "snail shells." *Rigate* refers to the ridges on the outside of the shells. We like this shape, especially for creamy sauces, because the sauce stays inside the shells. The ridges also hold the sauce on the outside.

Farfalle with Pancetta, Chickpeas, and Saffron
Farfalle con Ceci e Pancetta

Serves 6

FARFALLE

The name of this pasta means "but–terflies," and suggests the shape of the pasta. Farfalle are often used for elegant pastas. They are delicate and make a beautiful dish.

1/3 pound dried chickpeas, covered with cool water and soaked overnight
1 carrot, cut into a few pieces
1/2 small white or yellow onion
1 small potato
1 teaspoon baking soda
1/3 cup extra virgin olive oil
1 garlic clove
1/2 pound pancetta (or bacon), cut into 1/2-inch strips
1/2 teaspoon cayenne pepper
1 tablespoon Fresh Tomato Sauce (page 9; or bottled sauce*)
1/2 teaspoon ground saffron (or a pinch of saffron threads)
1 tablespoon sugar (or more to taste)
Salt and freshly ground black pepper
1 pound farfalle
2 tablespoons finely chopped fresh Italian parsley
Freshly grated Parmesan cheese

See source list.

Chickpeas are a very basic food in Sicily—we call them ceci (pronounced "CHE-chi"). They are something that you can have in the pantry, which made them a staple in the days before we had refrigerators. There is a very funny story about a pharmacist in town. He was very cheap. Everyone in Gangi has a little piece of land on which they plant a little bit of favas, a little bit of tomatoes, things they were used to growing from the days when they lived in the country. This man was famous for planting only ceci because he was sure to be able to save them—none would go to waste. The result was that his family had to eat ceci all through the year. Traditionally, ceci are made into soup but we like them so much, we thought we'd toss them into pastasciutta.

1. Drain the soaked chickpeas in a colander and rinse them with cool water. Place them in a big soup pot with the carrot pieces, the onion half, and the potato. Fill the pot with cool water and bring the water to a boil. When the water is boiling, take the pot off the heat and stir in the baking soda. (We add baking soda because we believe it makes the chickpeas tender and creamy inside. But if you do this while the pot is on the heat, the water will bubble up like mad.) Put the pot back on the heat and bring the water back to a boil. Reduce the heat and simmer the chickpeas for 2 to 3 hours, until they are tender and creamy inside. While the beans are simmering, scrape off any foam that forms on the top of the pot. The foam is the bitterness cooking out of the beans—it's as if the chickpeas are purifying themselves. When the chickpeas are tender and creamy but not mushy—you want to be able to feel them on your teeth—they're done. Leave the chickpeas in the water until you are ready to use them; otherwise they will dry out.

2. Heat the oil in a large frying pan over low heat. Add the garlic clove and the pancetta and sauté for 2 to 3 minutes, until the garlic is fragrant and the pancetta is beginning to brown. Add the hot pepper, tomato sauce, saffron, sugar, and 2 tablespoons of water and cook over a low flame for 10 minutes, until the pancetta is cooked. Remove the garlic and add salt, pepper, and more sugar to taste. Drain the chickpeas in a colander, add them to the frying pan, and sauté the chickpeas with the pancetta for about 10 minutes so the flavors come together.

3. In the meantime, bring a large saucepan of water to a boil. Add a small fistful of salt and the farfalle and cook until the pasta is tender. Reserve some of the pasta water, then drain the farfalle quickly in a colander and put it back in the saucepan you cooked it in. Add the prepared *condimento* and some hot pasta water and mix well over very high heat for about 2 minutes, adding more pasta water if the pasta is dry or sticky. Transfer the pasta to a pasta bowl. Sprinkle with the parsley. Serve hot, with grated Parmesan cheese on the table.

TIP The tendency is to undercook dried beans. You must cook them long enough so that they are not just tender, but soft and creamy in the center.

TIP If you sprinkle cheese on the pasta and then waste time before serving it, the cheese absorbs the liquid in the *condimento* and the pasta becomes very dry.

Homemade specialties at one of our local shops

TIP If the oil sizzles when you add the garlic, it's too hot. Take the pan off the fire to cool before adding the garlic.

1 pound fresh salmon, cut into
 1/2-inch cubes
1 large handful wild or domestic
 fennel leaves
Juice of 1 lemon
Salt and freshly ground black pepper
1/2 cup extra virgin olive oil
1 garlic clove
1 long sprig fresh rosemary
1 pound sedanini
1 cup toasted breadcrumbs mixed
 with a pinch of cayenne pepper

SEDANINI RIGATE
are short tubes with ridges on the outside, like penne, but without the pointed ends. We use sedanini with any creamy *condimento* or pesto that will stay inside the tubes.

Maria's Sedanini with Salmon, Fennel, and Rosemary
Sedanini al Profumo di Mare di Maria

Serves 6

I love salmon. It is one of my favorite fish, and I think that the taste of salmon with wild fennel is perfect. Maria is my auntie, my mamma's sister. She makes this especially for me. —G.

TIP Tie your fennel together into a bunch so that it's easy to lift out and toss when you're done marinating the fish.

1. Put the salmon, fennel, lemon juice, salt, and pepper in a bowl and let it sit at room temperature for about 2 hours to marinate.
2. Heat the olive oil in a large frying pan over medium heat. Add the garlic and rosemary and sauté for a minute or two until you smell the garlic. Lift the salmon out of the marinade with your hands and place it in the frying pan. Sauté the fish for 1 or 2 minutes, until it is opaque. (The lemon juice "cooked" the salmon, so you are just heating it to give it the flavor of the oil and a little color.) Add salt and pepper to taste.
3. In the meantime, bring a large saucepan of water to a boil. Stir in a small fistful of salt and the sedanini. Cook the pasta, stirring occasionally so it doesn't stick together, until it is tender. Reserve a cupful of the pasta water. Drain the pasta quickly through a colander and add it to the frying pan with the salmon. Add a splash of pasta water and sauté the pasta with the salmon *condimento* for 2 minutes on high heat. Transfer the pasta to a serving dish, sprinkle with the toasted breadcrumbs, and serve very hot with more breadcrumbs on the table.

LEFTOVER PASTA

When we have leftover pasta, we do not try to resuscitate it into the life it had before. Instead, we turn it into something else altogether: fried spaghetti. It is delicious—crunchy on the outside, and like a pasta pie on the inside. We also try bavette or linguine. *Bucatini con le sarde* is one pasta dish we eat fried quite often. In truth, if you are not bound by tradition, you could fry any pasta you like. Heat oil or butter in a nonstick frying pan. Add the spaghetti and fry until it is golden brown and crusty. Turn and fry until the other side is golden. Serve sliced.

The other way we use leftover spaghetti is to make a frittata. First, put the pasta in a bowl and toss it with enough fresh tomato sauce so that it is not dry. Beat 2 eggs (for roughly 1/2 pound of pasta) and pour over the spaghetti. Mix very well and put in a hot frying pan with oil or butter. Fry until golden and crunchy on both sides. Serve sliced.

TOASTED BREADCRUMBS

in Sicily are often used as the poor man's Parmesan. To toast bread-crumbs, heat enough olive oil to cover the bottom of a small frying pan over medium-low heat. Add the breadcrumbs (stale bread that has been ground in a blender or food processor) and toast them, stirring often so they don't burn, until the crumbs are a rich, golden brown, adding a little more oil whenever the breadcrumbs look dry. A ratio of 1 cup of breadcrumbs to 2 tablespoons of oil is a good measure to begin with. But here at Gangivecchio, we do not measure breadcrumbs. We simply grind up all of our stale bread, keep the crumbs in an airtight container in the pantry, and scoop some out whenever we need them. We use them untoasted for coating a tim-ballo pan and toasted for serving on pasta. If you are making a seafood pasta, you can use the oil from the anchovy bottle for very fishy-tasting breadcrumbs. If you like spicy food, add a pinch of cayenne pepper to the breadcrumbs.

Sedanini Rigate with Summer Vegetable Puree
Sedanini Rigate con Crema di Verdure

Serves 6

With all the vegetables coming from the home garden at Gangivecchio, this is a sort of welcome-to-summertime dish. It may seem like a lot of vegetables, but they reduce when they are cooked and become sweet and delicious. You can use any fresh herbs you want. We like the combination of mint and basil in this dish.

1 pound eggplant
1/2 cup extra virgin olive oil
2 garlic cloves, chopped
1 pound red and yellow bell peppers,
  cored, seeds and pith removed,
  and diced
1 pound zucchini, diced
One 10–ounce can whole peeled
  tomatoes, drained in a colander
  and torn apart with your hands
1 tablespoon sugar (or more to taste)
1/2 teaspoon cayenne pepper or hot
  pepper flakes
Salt and freshly ground black pepper
1 pound sedanini rigate
1 teaspoon chopped fresh rosemary
8–10 fresh basil leaves, torn into
  small pieces
8–10 fresh mint leaves, torn into
  small pieces
Freshly grated Parmesan cheese

1. Cut the skin off the eggplant with a paring knife and dice the egg–plant.

2. Heat the oil and the garlic cloves together in a large frying pan over medium heat until the garlic begins to be fragrant but is not brown. Add the eggplant, peppers, and zucchini and sauté for 10 to 15 minutes, until the vegetables are tender. Add the tomatoes, sugar, hot pepper, and salt and pepper to taste and simmer for about 45 minutes, until the peppers are very tender and the zucchini is falling apart. Add a splash of water (hot pasta water if the pasta is cooking) from time to time if the vegeta–bles are sticking to the pan. Taste for salt and sugar and season with more to taste.

3. Pour the vegetables and cooking juices into the bowl of a food processor fitted with a metal blade and puree until creamy. Return the pureed vegetables to the frying pan and keep warm over very low heat.

4. Meanwhile, bring a large saucepan of water to a boil. Stir in a small fistful of salt and the sedanini and cook, stirring occasionally, until the pasta is tender. Reserve a cupful of the hot pasta water. Drain the sedanini quickly through a colander, and transfer it to the frying pan with the pureed vegetables. Mix the pasta with the *condimento* very well over high heat for about 2 minutes, adding pasta water until the pasta is moist and slippery. Turn off the heat and stir in half of the rosemary, basil, and mint. Transfer the pasta to a serving bowl, sprinkle with the remaining herbs, and serve hot, with Parmesan on the table.

TIP We like to tear leafy herbs like basil and mint with our hands rather than chop them. Knives tend to impart a steely taste, and the taste of the herb is compromised.

Festonate with Gorgonzola, Mascarpone, and Walnuts
Festonate con Gorgonzola, Mascarpone e Noci

Serves 6

Gorgonzola cheese is one of our family favorites. The legend is that it was born by acci-dent. A shepherd in the north of Italy wanted to save some cheese, so he put it in a cave. He forgot about it for months, and when he went back for it, it was green, com-pletely covered in mold. He was terrified and thought all his cheeses were gone, ruined. But he decided to take a taste and discovered that inside, it was great, creamy and deli-cious. After eating this rich pasta, the only thing you will want is a crisp green salad.

TIP We add soybean oil or another mild–flavored oil to pasta water when we don't want the strong flavor of olive oil in a dish.

1. Bring a large saucepan of water to a boil. Stir in a small fistful of salt and a splash of oil. Add the pasta and stir immediately with a long fork to keep it from sticking together. Boil the pasta until it is tender.

2. While the pasta is cooking, place the gorgonzola and mascarpone in a big serving bowl and mash them together with a fork. When the pasta is halfway done cooking, pour about 1 cup of the hot pasta water into the bowl with the cheese and stir until it is smooth. Add more hot pasta water until it is about the consistency of buttermilk. Stir in the walnuts, Parmesan cheese, salt to taste, and hot pepper. Cover the serving bowl with a cloth or a plate to keep the cheese warm while the pasta cooks.

3. When the festonate is tender, reserve a cupful of the pasta water and drain the pasta quickly in a colander.

4. Put the festonate into the bowl with the cheese and a splash of pasta water. Toss the pasta with the *condimento* using a pair of tongs or forks. If the pasta is sticky, add more of the reserved pasta water until you have a smooth sauce coating the pasta. Serve immediately. Pass the Parmesan.

TIP We don't like to use a food processor to chop nuts, because it turns them into dust. Instead, we use a mezzaluna, a half–moon cutter that rocks back and forth on a cutting board. It works very quickly and chops very fine.

Salt for the pasta water
Soybean oil (or other mild–flavored oil) for the pasta water and for deep–frying
1 pound festonate
1/2 cup sweet gorgonzola cheese
1/2 cup mascarpone cheese
1 1/2 cups walnuts, chopped superfine
1/3 cup (about 1 ounce) grated Parme-san cheese, plus more for passing at the table
1/2 teaspoon cayenne pepper

FESTONATE
means "streamers," like the ones used to decorate a ballroom for a holiday. They are long, with a rib-boned edge. It is a festive shape that reminds us of music and dancing. We twirl it on our fork the way we would spaghetti. But if Americans have trouble twirling spaghetti, I can't imagine what they will do with these long wide streamers. You may want to break the festonate in half before boiling it.

La Cambusa's Linguine with Shrimp, Zucchini, and Cherry Tomatoes
Le Linguine con Gamberi, Zucchine e Pomodorini della Cambusa

Serves 6

TIP It's important to use small shrimp in this pasta, so that it fits whole on your fork when you twirl the pasta. American shrimp are giants—they're really good, but so big. Try to find those that have been dieting for all their lives.

La Cambusa is one of our favorite restaurants in Palermo. It is in the Piazza Marina, an elegant plaza in one of the oldest neighborhoods in Palermo. La Cambusa has such a beautiful antipasto selection that we rarely eat pasta there. But our coauthor, Carolina, tried this dish one night. We all had a bite, and we liked it so much, we asked if we could include it in the book. We know very well that it is rare for an Italian cook or restaurant owner to give you a correct recipe without leaving out an important ingredient. But I promised Paolo, the owner of La Cambusa, that I would have to kill him if it wasn't right. He answered that he would give me a perfect recipe and save me from jail. —G.

TIP Do not sauté garlic on high heat. If you do, it will burn, and burned garlic is very bitter.

Salt
1 pound small shrimp in the shell
1/2 cup extra virgin olive oil, plus more for the pasta water
A walnut of butter (about 2 tablespoons)
2 garlic cloves
1/2 pound cherry tomatoes, cut in half
Freshly ground black pepper
1 zucchini, thinly sliced
1 pound linguine
1/2 cup finely chopped fresh Italian parsley

1. Bring a medium saucepan of water to a boil. Add a pinch of salt and the shrimp, and boil until the shrimp are just tender. Drain the shrimp in a colander and allow them to cool. When the shrimp are cool enough to touch, remove and discard the shells.

2. In a large frying pan, heat the oil and butter with the garlic cloves over medium heat for 2 to 3 minutes, until the garlic is fragrant and light golden brown. Add the cherry tomatoes and salt and pepper to taste and sauté for about 3 minutes, or until the tomatoes begin to soften and give off juice. Add the zucchini slices and sauté for another few minutes, until they are soft but not falling apart. Add the boiled shrimp and cook on medium heat just to integrate the flavors. Turn off the heat and save the *condimento* in the frying pan.

3. Meanwhile, bring a large saucepan of water to a boil and add a small fistful of salt and a splash of olive oil. Add the linguine and stir so that it doesn't stick together. When the linguine is al dente, lift it out with a *scola spaghetti* and into the frying pan with the shrimp and zucchini. Sauté with a splash of hot pasta water over high heat for 1 minute or until very hot and well mixed. Transfer the linguine to a serving bowl, sprinkle with the parsley, and serve immediately.

Paolo's Pennette with Fresh Figs and Pancetta
Pennette con Fichi e Pancetta di Paolo

Serves 6

This is a recipe my brother invented, inspired from the fact that every day during the fall he walks out of his apartment at Gangivecchio to see the tons of fresh figs that have dropped off the two giant trees in the center of our courtyard. It's nice to serve this pasta with an additional whole fig, cut in quarters so that it opens like a flower with the contrast of the green peel and the red condimento.

1. Heat the olive oil in a large frying pan over medium–high heat until it is hot but not smoking. Add the onions and sauté for a few minutes until they begin to soften. Add the pancetta and cook until the pancetta and the onions are golden brown, 7 to 10 minutes. Add the figs and the wine and simmer just to soften the figs, about 5 minutes; don't cook the figs so long that they fall apart completely. Season with salt and pepper to taste and turn off the heat.

2. Meanwhile, bring a big saucepan of water to a boil. Stir in a small fistful of salt and the pennette and cook until it is tender. Reserve a cupful of the pasta water and drain the pasta in a colander.

3. Quickly transfer the pasta to the pan with the figs and place over high heat. Add a splash of pasta water, stir gently to mix the *condimento* and pasta together, and sauté for 2 to 3 minutes, adding more pasta water if the pasta is dry or sticky. Serve hot with freshly grated Parmesan cheese at the table.

TIP Peeling figs is very easy. Just pull the skin right off with your fingers.

1/2 cup extra virgin olive oil
1 medium white onion, finely chopped
1/4 pound pancetta (or bacon), cut into 1/2-inch cubes
2 pounds fresh figs, peeled and diced
1/2 cup dry red wine
Salt and freshly ground black pepper
1 pound pennette
Freshly grated Parmesan cheese

Bucato with a Carnival of Sweet Peppers
Bucato con Carnevale di Peperoni Dolci

This pasta is as beautiful to look at as it is to eat. I tried this recipe for the first time with our coauthor, Carolina. It was a happy surprise for both of us: for me because until that moment, I had just written the recipe, not made it, and for her, because until she tasted it, she couldn't have had any faith in such a mess of ingredients. —W.

3/4 cup extra virgin olive oil
3 yellow bell peppers, cored, seeds and pith removed, and thinly sliced
3 red bell peppers, cored, seeds and pith removed, and thinly sliced
3 green bell peppers, cored, seeds and pith removed, and thinly sliced
Salt and freshly ground black pepper
1 tablespoon sugar (or more to taste)
1 cup veal or beef broth
1 pound bucato, strands broken in half
1 cup (about 1 1/2 ounces) shaved Parmesan cheese, plus more, grated, for passing at the table
2 tablespoons finely chopped fresh Italian parsley

1. Heat the oil in a large frying pan over medium heat. Add the peppers and stir frequently so they don't stick and burn. After a few minutes, add the salt and pepper, sugar, and a spoonful of water and lower the heat. Continue to cook for a few minutes. When the peppers begin to be tender, taste one to see if you want to add more sugar or salt. Add the broth and cook the peppers until most of the broth is evaporated and the peppers are very tender and sweet and dark around some of the edges, about 20 minutes. Add more water from time to time if the pan is dry.

2. Meanwhile, bring a large saucepan of water to a boil. Stir in a small fistful of salt and the bucato. When the pasta is tender, reserve a cupful of the pasta water and drain the pasta quickly in a colander. Return the pasta to the pot you cooked it in and add the peppers and any liquid in the pan. Add 1/4 cup of the reserved pasta water. Crush the Parmesan shavings between the palms of your hands over the pasta. Add the parsley and toss it all together over high heat for 1 minute. Add a little more pasta water if the pasta is sticky. Serve very hot. Pass the Parmesan.

A colorful tangle of sweet peppers and pasta

Shells with Fresh Fava Beans and Ricotta
Conchiglie con Fave Fresche e Ricotta

Serves 6

Favas are best when they are so young you only have to shell them once. Later in the season, the outer skin gets tough, and after shelling them you must parboil the beans and remove the skin from the individual beans. This isn't difficult, but is very tedious work. This recipe is for young favas, so find them if you can, but if yours are on the large side, parboil the beans and peel them.

1. Heat the oil in a large frying pan over medium heat. Add the onions and sauté for 3 to 4 minutes, until they begin to soften. Add the shelled fava beans and salt and pepper to taste. Reduce the heat to low, add 1 cup of water, and cook until the favas are tender. The amount of time this takes will vary from between 20 to 35 minutes, depending on the size of the favas. Add water if the pan is dry and the favas are sticking. When the favas are tender to the bite, turn off the heat.

2. Meanwhile, put the fresh ricotta with 2 tablespoons hot water in the bowl you will serve the pasta in. Mash the ricotta with a fork and add water, if necessary, until the ricotta has a creamy consistency. Add salt and pepper to taste and mix again.

3. Place a quarter of the cooked fava beans in the bowl of a food processor fitted with a metal blade and run the processor until the favas are completely pureed. Add the fava puree to the bowl with the ricotta and mix them together well. Place a walnut of butter on top of the ricotta–fava cream. (It will melt when you toss it with the hot pasta.)

4. Bring a large saucepan of water to boil. Stir in a small fistful of salt and the conchiglie and boil until tender. Reserve a cupful of the pasta water and drain the shells in a colander. Put the pasta and a splash of the reserved pasta water in the serving bowl with the ricotta–fava cream and toss, adding more pasta water if the pasta appears dry or sticky, so that the shells are coated with the cream. Place the remaining whole favas on top of the pasta, sprinkle with the grated pecorino, and serve immediately with more grated pecorino on the table.

In the springtime, fava beans are abundant in markets and home gardens. We look for those that are small; these are younger and will be more tender.

CONCHIGLIE
are big shells. They catch a lot of sauce and small vegetables inside, so we like to use them with small vegetables. Be careful when you taste them for doneness—they also catch a lot of boiling water!

1 cup extra virgin olive oil
1 small onion, finely chopped
3 pounds fresh fava beans, shelled (about 1 1/2 cups shelled beans)
Salt and freshly ground black pepper
3/4 pound fresh ricotta*
1 pound conchiglie
A walnut of butter (about 2 table-spoons)
1/4 cup grated pecorino cheese, plus more for passing at the table

See source list.

Ditalini with Creamed Winter Squash and Nutmeg
Ditalini con Crema di Zucca Rossa d'Inverno

Serves 6

During the promotional tour for our second book, we bought many vegetable seeds in America to grow at Gangivecchio. Some combination of the California seeds and the Sicilian sun gave us winter squash so big we couldn't get our arms around them. That year every friend, relative, and visitor left Gangivecchio with a monster yellow squash in their arms. Even the taxman who paid us a visit: "You like squash? Good! Here!" We stored the thousands we had left downstairs in an ancient room in the abbey. This recipe was one of many delicious ways we discovered to make use of the abundance of squash.

1 small onion, peeled
1 pound winter squash (such as pumpkin, hubbard, or butternut)
Salt
1 1/2 cups extra virgin olive oil
8 tablespoons (1 stick) unsalted butter
1/2 teaspoon cayenne pepper or hot pepper flakes
1/2 teaspoon freshly grated nutmeg
Freshly ground black pepper
1 pound ditalini
1/2 cup (about 1 1/2 ounces) grated Parmesan cheese, plus more for passing at the table

1. Boil the onion for about 15 to 20 minutes, until it is tender when pierced with a toothpick or fork. Drain and mince the onion.

2. Peel the squash with a very sharp knife. Cut the squash in half and scoop out and discard the seeds and pulp inside. Cut three-quarters of the squash into 1-inch cubes. Cut the remaining quarter of the squash into 1/4-inch-thick slices. Place the squash cubes in a large saucepan of lightly salted boiling water and boil until they are tender when pierced with a fork. Drain through a colander. When they're cool enough to work with, puree them in a food mill or the bowl of a food processor fitted with a metal blade.

3. Heat 1/2 cup of the olive oil with 2 tablespoons of the butter in a frying pan on medium-high heat. Add the squash slices and fry them until they are golden brown on both sides. Remove the squash from the oil and place them on paper towels to drain.

4. Add the minced onion and the remaining oil and butter to the frying pan you fried the squash slices in and sauté over medium heat until the onion is translucent and light golden, about 5 minutes. Add the pureed squash, hot pepper, nutmeg, and salt and pepper to taste, and cook over low heat, adding a little pasta water if the pan is dry and the squash is sticking, for 5 minutes until the squash is warmed through.

5. Meanwhile, bring a large saucepan of water to a boil. Stir in a small fistful of salt and the ditalini. Boil the pasta, stirring from time to time, until tender. Reserve a cupful of the pasta water and drain the pasta quickly through a colander. Add the drained pasta to the frying pan with the squash. (If the frying pan is not big enough, put the pasta back in the pot you cooked it in and add the pureed squash to that pot.) Stir in the grated Parmesan cheese and enough pasta water so that you have a smooth sauce and the pasta is not sticky. Stir all the ingredients together and cook over high heat for about 2 minutes, adding more pasta water if necessary.

6. Transfer to a serving bowl. Top with the fried squash slices and a sprinkling of Parmesan. Serve immediately and pass the Parmesan.

TIP Boiling onion takes the burning quality out of it, and leaves only the sweet onion taste.

Tagliatelline with Pancetta, Mint, and a Rainbow of Summer Vegetables
Arcobaleno di Tagliatelline

Serves 6

The rainbow is something that I like because it reminds me of the American song "Somewhere Over the Rainbow." When I was a child, I would look at a rainbow and I was sure that it was something real, with a beginning and an end, and I thought I knew exactly where the end of the rainbow was. —G.

6 fresh mint leaves

3 anchovy fillets in oil

1/4 cup extra virgin olive oil, plus more for the pasta water

1/4 pound pancetta (or bacon), cut into 1/2-inch strips

1 medium white or yellow onion, minced

3 garlic cloves, minced

1/2 pound red bell peppers, halved, seeds and pith removed, and diced

1/2 pound (about 3 small) zucchini, diced

1/4 pound green beans, cleaned, trimmed, and cut into 1-inch pieces

1/2 cup black olives, pitted and chopped

One 10-ounce can peeled whole tomatoes, drained in a colander

1 teaspoon dried oregano

2 cups veal or beef broth

Salt and freshly ground black pepper

1 pound tagliatelline

1/2 cup (about 1 1/2 ounces) freshly grated Parmesan cheese, plus more for passing at the table

1. Mince the mint leaves with the anchovies and set aside.

2. Warm the oil in a large sauté pan with high sides over medium-high heat. Add the pancetta and sauté until it begins to brown. Lower the heat and add the onions, garlic, bell pepper, zucchini, green beans, olives, and the minced anchovies and mint. Cook until the onions and peppers are very tender, 15 to 20 minutes, adding a little water from time to time when the vegetables are sticking to the pan or sizzling.

3. Add the tomatoes, breaking them up with your hands over the pan, and sauté for a few minutes, to allow the tomatoes to integrate with the rest of the vegetables and warm through. Sprinkle the vegetables with the oregano, pour the broth into the pan, and simmer the vegetables over low heat for another 30 minutes, adding more water if necessary to have a smooth, not sticky, *condimento*. Add salt and pepper to taste.

4. While the vegetables are simmering, bring a large saucepan of water to a boil. Stir in a small fistful of salt and a splash of olive oil. Add the tagliatelline and immediately stir with a long fork so that the strands don't stick together. Boil the pasta, stirring often, until it is al dente.

5. Lift the tagliatelline out of the water and into the sauté pan with the *condimento* using a *scola spaghetti*. Add a splash of pasta water and sprinkle half of the Parmesan cheese over the pasta. Picking the pasta up with two forks, mix it with the vegetables over high heat for a couple of minutes until the pasta is coated with the *condimento*, adding more pasta water if the pasta is sticky; the tagliatelline should be slippery and smooth. Transfer to a pasta bowl, sprinkle the remaining Parmesan over the top, and serve hot, with more Parmesan on the table.

Casareccia with Zucchini and Its Flowers
Casareccia con Fiori di Zucca

Serves 6

One of the masterpieces of our home garden is zucchini and its flowers. In August, Peppe starts his harvest. For the first few days, we are very happy and find a million ways new and old to cook the zucchini flowers. This is one of our family favorites that we make even after we are otherwise tired of the flowers.

1. Warm the oil and butter in a large saucepan over low heat until the butter melts. Add the chopped zucchini flowers and sauté over low heat until they begin to soften, about 3 minutes. Remove the flowers from the pan and set aside.

2. Add the onions to the pan you cooked the zucchini flowers in and cook over medium heat until they are tender and translucent, 7 to 10 minutes. Add the zucchini and cook until tender, about 5 minutes. Pour the chicken broth into the pan and let it simmer until the *condimento* is creamy, 30 to 40 minutes.

3. Drain the vegetables, reserving both the vegetables and the broth. Pour the broth back into the saucepan and add enough water to cook the pasta. Bring to a boil, add a small fistful of salt, stir in the casareccia, and cook until the pasta is tender.

4. Meanwhile, place the vegetables in a large frying pan and stir in the boiled egg yolks, half of the caciocavallo cheese, and salt and pepper to taste.

5. When the pasta is tender, reserve a cupful of the pasta water and drain the pasta quickly in a colander. Transfer the drained pasta along with 1/2 cup of pasta water to the frying pan with the vegetables. Stir them together over high heat until the *condimento* is heated through, about 2 minutes. Add more pasta water if the pasta is sticky. Transfer to a serving bowl, sprinkle with the remaining caciocavallo, and serve hot, with grated Parmesan on the table.

1/2 cup extra virgin olive oil
4 tablespoons (1/2 stick) unsalted butter
15 zucchini flowers, cleaned, stamens removed, and coarsely chopped
1 medium white or yellow onion, diced
2 small zucchini, diced
5 cups chicken broth
Salt
1 pound casareccia (gemelli) or penne
2 hard-boiled egg yolks, smashed with a fork
1/3 cup (1 ounce) grated caciocavallo cheese (or provolone)
Freshly ground black pepper
Freshly grated Parmesan cheese

CASARECCIA
means "homemade," but we use the word to describe the dry version of a shape that was traditionally handmade. It is also called *gemelli*, which means "twins," because the shape looks like two short strands of spaghetti twisted together. It is the shape we always use for our Five-Nut Pesto (page 51), and other thick *condimenti*.

Farfalle with Springtime Vegetables and Pecorino Cheese
Farfalle Primavera

Serves 4

1 1/4 cups extra virgin olive oil
2 garlic cloves
1/2 pound frozen or fresh shelled green peas
4 asparagus spears, trimmed and cut into 1-inch pieces
12 green beans, trimmed and cut into 1-inch pieces
2 celery stalks, cut into 1/2-inch pieces
2 scallions, minced (white part only)
4 small zucchini, cut into 1/2-inch cubes
4 small carrots, halved and cut into 1/2-inch pieces
2 large tomatoes, peeled, seeded, and cubed
Salt and freshly ground black pepper
1 pound farfalle
1/4 cup finely chopped fresh Italian parsley
1/3 cup (about 1 ounce) grated pecorino cheese, plus more for the table

In Sicily, in addition to cultivated asparagus, which is the asparagus that most people are familiar with, we also have wild asparagus that grows in the springtime, hidden away under the bushes. You have to wear high boots and gloves and cover your face when you look for it, otherwise you will come out with 400 scratches all over your face for the 12 asparagus you found. The wild asparagus are tall and long, like spaghetti, and they twirl around on a plant. They taste like cultivated asparagus but with a bigger back taste of the forest.

1. Heat 1 cup of the oil in a large frying pan over low heat. Add the garlic and sauté for 2 minutes, until it is fragrant. Add the peas, asparagus, green beans, celery, scallions, zucchini, and carrots. Increase the heat to high and sauté the vegetables for 5 to 6 minutes, until they soften. Add the tomatoes and cook for another 5 minutes. Season with salt and pepper to taste.

2. Meanwhile, bring a medium saucepan of water to a boil. Stir in a small fistful of salt and the farfalle and cook until tender. Reserve a cupful of the pasta water and drain the pasta in a colander.

3. Add the pasta, 1/2 cup of the reserved pasta water, and the remaining 1/4 cup of oil to the frying pan with the vegetables. Sauté the pasta and *condimento* together for a few minutes to blend all the flavors. Add the parsley and the pecorino cheese. Mix well and serve very hot, with more grated pecorino on the table.

A woman sells produce at the weekly market in Gangi.

"Straw and Hay" with Green Peas and Lettuce in Prosciutto Cream Sauce
Paglia e Fieno con Piselli e Lattuga

Serves 6

This is the kind of rich, creamy-sauce pasta that Americans seem to love. We like it, too, though we rarely use cream in our cooking. We do say that cream is the best "doctor" in the kitchen—a little cream can fix any sauce. But this sauce was born with cream—it is not there to cover up a mistake, just to make the peas and lettuce even sweeter than they are.

1. Bring a big saucepan of water to a boil and cook the peas until just tender, about 3 minutes. Drain the peas in a colander and set them aside.

2. Warm the oil and butter in a large frying pan over medium heat. Add the scallions and sauté until they wilt and turn light golden, about 5 minutes. Add the broth and wine and bring to a simmer. Add the tomato sauce and peas, return to a simmer, and cook for about 5 minutes, to soften the peas and meld the flavors. Season with salt and pepper to taste. Add the shredded lettuce and the ham and cook just to wilt the lettuce and warm the ham, about 5 minutes.

3. Meanwhile, bring a saucepan of water to a boil. Stir in a fistful of salt and a splash of olive oil. Put the pasta in the water. Use a long pasta fork to stir the pasta just after putting it in the water and occasionally while it's cooking so that the strands of pasta don't stick together. Boil the pasta until al dente and use a spaghetti strainer to lift the pasta out of the pot and into the frying pan with the *condimento*, reserving the pasta water. Add the cream and a splash of pasta water and stir the pasta and *condimento* together over high heat for about 2 minutes. Add more pasta water if the strands are sticking together. Transfer the pasta to a serving dish, sprinkle with Parmesan cheese, and serve immediately, with more grated Parmesan on the table.

1/2 pound frozen or fresh shelled green peas
1/3 cup extra virgin olive oil, plus more for the pasta water
A walnut of butter (about 2 tablespoons)
2 scallions, minced (white part only)
1/4 cup vegetable broth
1 cup dry white wine
1 tablespoon Fresh Tomato Sauce (page 9; or bottled sauce*)
Salt and freshly ground black pepper
1/2 head butter lettuce, torn into thin shreds
5 ounces prosciutto cotto (cooked ham), cubed
1 pound paglia e fieno (or 1/2 pound linguine and 1/2 pound spinach linguine)
1/2 cup heavy cream
Freshly grated Parmesan cheese

*See source list.

PAGLIA E FIENO, which means "straw and hay," is a specialty in Italy. It gets its name from the color. It is a combination of semolina and spinach linguine. The semolina linguine is the straw. The green spinach linguine is the hay. You can find paglia e fieno both fresh and dried.

Rigatoni with Swordfish Ragù
Rigatoni con Ragù di Pesce Spada

Serves 6

comes from the word *rigate*, which means "ridged." It is a pasta shape that we like to toss with a rich sauce, use in a baked pasta with *ragù*, or fry as a leftover. It is the only type of pasta we will not eat with just garlic and oil. Rigatoni is too big; it needs sauce.

1/2 cup extra virgin olive oil
2 scallions, cleaned and minced (white and light green parts)
3/4 pound swordfish, cut into 1-inch cubes
1 cup dry white wine
Pinch of saffron threads or powder
Juice and grated zest of 1/2 lemon
Salt and freshly ground black pepper
1 pound rigatoni
4 tablespoons capers, rinsed
1/3 cup coarsely chopped fresh marjoram

Swordfish is one of Sicily's favorite fish. It's not the most expensive, nor is it considered the fanciest. But it is one of our favorites. We say "ragù" when something is cooked for a long time in a skillet with liquid and other flavors, which this dish is.

TIP People tend to undercook rigatoni. To test rigatoni, take a piece out of the water and cut it in half. If you see a chalky white line in the pasta, keep cooking it. Otherwise you will be chewing forever.

1. Warm the olive oil with 2 tablespoons of water in a large frying pan over low heat. Add the scallions and sauté for 5 minutes or until they are very soft and translucent. Add the swordfish cubes and sauté, turning them from time to time, until they are light golden brown on all sides. Add the wine, saffron, and lemon juice and cook for another 5 minutes. Season with salt and pepper to taste. Turn off the heat.
2. Meanwhile, bring a large saucepan of water to a boil. Stir in a small fistful of salt and the rigatoni and cook until the rigatoni is tender. Reserve a cupful of the pasta water and drain the rigatoni quickly in a colander.
3. When the rigatoni is almost done, put the frying pan with the sword-fish back on low heat. Add the capers, grated lemon zest, and marjoram, stir together, and cook for about 2 minutes, adding pasta water to the pan if it is dry.
4. Put the drained rigatoni in the frying pan with the swordfish *ragù* over high heat. Add a splash of pasta water and sauté the pasta with the *ragù* for 1 to 2 minutes, stirring to coat the pasta with the sauce and adding more pasta water until the pasta is wet and slippery. Transfer the rigatoni to a serving dish. Top with freshly ground black pepper and serve immediately.

Ditalini Cooked like Risotto with Wild Mushrooms
Ditalini come Risotto

Serves 6

One afternoon, my English friend Claire came over. She was very distraught because her son's girlfriend was coming from Rome and she didn't have anything to feed her. I had just made this pasta—something I had invented in a daydream and wanted to try cooking. I baked it in a tube pan (something you can do, but we don't call for that in this recipe because it is best fresh from the pot), and left it in the pan. I gave it to her so that she just had to go home and put it in the oven to warm it. She told me she had so many compliments. Claire doesn't cook, but she is very honest. When she served the dish and her guests told her how beautiful it was, she told them that I had made it. —G.

1. Lift the porcini out of the water they are soaking in and drain them well, reserving the water. Coarsely chop the porcini.

2. Warm the oil in a large frying pan over low heat. Add the garlic and sauté until it is aromatic and light golden, 3 to 4 minutes. Add the chopped portobello and porcini mushrooms to the pan and sauté over medium heat until they are tender. Transfer the mushrooms and pan juices to a bowl and set aside.

3. In the same frying pan over medium heat, melt the butter with the broth. Add the minced scallions and sauté until they begin to soften and get some color. Stir in the parsley and the salt and pepper to taste. Add the ditalini and stir to mix. Add a cupful of warm water and the saffron and continue to cook, stirring constantly as you would risotto, adding more water when the water in the pan has evaporated and you can hear the pasta sizzling.

4. After you have added 2 cups of water, add the mushrooms and pan juices and the porcini water. Continue to cook, adding more water if necessary, until the pasta is al dente. Stir in the Parmesan cheese. Transfer the pasta to a serving dish. Sprinkle with more grated Parmesan and serve hot, passing the Parmesan.

"I like to say that my mother would make it through a war: she never has less than ten pounds of butter in the refrigerator, and I don't know how many bags of pasta in the drawers. One very snowy winter a few years ago, nobody was able to leave home. All the roads were closed. After a few days, a woman who lives down the road came to the house asking if we had any food. Of course we did. My mamma decided that she and I would make pasta and take it around to all of the neighbors. During hard times, people are nicer to each other. I think it is because we realize how fragile we are."

—G.

4 ounces dried porcini mushrooms, soaked in 2 cups of warm water for 30 minutes

1/2 cup extra virgin olive oil

4 garlic cloves, minced

1/4 pound portobello mushrooms, cleaned and coarsely chopped

10 tablespoons (1 1/4 sticks) unsalted butter

4 cups chicken broth, simmering

2 scallions, minced (white part only)

1/3 cup finely chopped fresh Italian parsley

Salt and freshly ground black pepper

1 pound ditalini

Pinch of saffron threads or powder

1/3 cup (about 1 ounce) freshly grated Parmesan cheese, plus more to pass at the table

Pappardelle with Asparagus, Walnuts, and Speck
Pappardelle con Asparagi, Noci e Speck

Serves 6

"In Sicily, we eat only the tip of the asparagus. In fact, this is a sign of proper behavior. If you have a good education, the nuns teach you how to eat certain things. They show you which fork to use for eating specific foods. Then there is the drama that says you can use a spoon only when eating soup, not when eating anything else. Even if a pasta shape is miniscule, if it is not in a soup, you must find a way to eat it with a fork."
—G.

8 tablespoons (1 stick) unsalted butter
3 fresh sage leaves
1/2 pound asparagus tips, cut in half and boiled until just tender
1/2 pound mascarpone cheese
2–4 tablespoons whole milk
1/4 pound walnuts, minced
1/3 pound speck, cut into cubes
Salt and freshly ground black pepper
Soybean oil (or other mild–flavored oil) for the pasta water
3/4 pound pappardelle
Freshly grated Parmesan cheese

If you find fresh fava beans at the market, they are great instead of or in addition to asparagus in this dish. We are not used to steaming vegetables; we boil them. If you are used to or prefer steaming, of course you could steam vegetables, like these asparagus, when we call for boiled.

TIP It is boring and tedious to crack nuts, but we find that they're so much better than the already shelled nuts, which often seem to be old and bitter.

1. Melt 4 tablespoons of the butter with a spoonful of water in a large frying pan over low heat. Add the sage and cook about 1 minute to flavor the butter. Add the asparagus and cook for 2 or 3 minutes. Take the pan off the heat and remove and discard the sage leaves.

2. Use a fork to mash the mascarpone with 2 tablespoons of the milk in a medium bowl. Add more milk if necessary to make a loose sauce. Stir in the walnuts and pour into the pan with the asparagus. Put the pan back on low heat, add the remaining butter, and cook until the *condimento* is creamy.

3. In a small frying pan, fry the speck for a few minutes until golden and slightly crispy. Add the fried speck to the pan with the mascarpone and asparagus. Adjust the seasoning with salt and pepper to taste and transfer to a pasta bowl.

4. Meanwhile, bring a saucepan of water to a boil. Stir in a small fistful of salt and a splash of oil. Add the pappardelle and cook, stirring often, until tender. Reserve a cupful of the pasta water and drain the pappardelle in a colander.

5. Quickly transfer the pappardelle to the pasta bowl. Mix the pasta with the *condimento* until it is coated, adding enough pasta water so the *condimento* is a nice, smooth consistency, coating the pappardelle. Sprinkle with Parmesan cheese and serve immediately with more Parmesan on the table.

Rigatoni with Fried Eggplant, Wild Fennel, and Fresh Sardines
Rigatoni con Melanzane Fritte, Finocchietti e Sarde

TIP Never fry different foods in the same oil. The oil becomes dirty and bitter.

Serves 4

This is a close relative of the pasta with sardines. The addition of eggplant is very Sicilian.

1. Pour enough flour on a plate to cover. Dredge the eggplant slices in the flour.

2. Pour enough olive oil in a large deep–frying pan to fill to 2 inches. Heat the oil over high heat until it is very hot but not smoking (a drop of water will sizzle when dropped in the oil). Place the floured eggplant slices in 1 layer in the pan; do not crowd. Fry until eggplant is golden brown on both sides, turning only once. Place the fried eggplant slices on a plate lined with paper towels to drain. Repeat with the remaining eggplant slices.

3. Open the sardines like a book. Pass each opened sardine through the flour until it is evenly coated. Pour enough safflower oil in a large frying pan to fill to 1 inch and warm over medium heat. Place the sardines in the pan to fry until they are golden brown on both sides, turning once. Remove the sardines from the oil and place them on a plate lined with paper towels to drain.

4. Bring a saucepan of water to a boil over high heat. Add a small fistful of salt and the fennel and blanch for about 5 minutes. Drain in a colander.

5. In a frying pan, heat the olive oil and garlic over medium heat and cook for about 2 minutes, until the garlic is fragrant and light golden. Remove the garlic and discard. Add the *estratto* and cook, breaking it up with a wooden spoon, until the *estratto* melts into the oil. Add the chopped fennel and sauté over medium heat for 10–15 minutes. Stir in the sugar and hot pepper. Add a few tablespoons of water and cook a few minutes longer. Adjust the salt and sugar to taste.

1 pound eggplant, sliced thin lengthwise

All–purpose flour for coating the eggplant and sardines

Olive oil for deep–frying

3/4 pound cleaned fresh sardines, rinsed under cool water and drained on paper towels

Safflower oil (or other mild–flavored oil) for frying the sardines

Salt

1 bunch wild fennel (or regular fennel fronds), finely chopped

1/4 cup extra virgin olive oil

2 garlic cloves

2 cups *estratto** (or tomato paste)

1 tablespoon sugar (or more to taste)

1 small hot red pepper, seeded and minced

3/4 pound rigatoni

Freshly grated Parmesan cheese

See source list.

6. Meanwhile, bring a big saucepan of water to a boil. Stir in a small fist-ful of salt and the rigatoni and cook until the pasta is tender. Save a cup-ful of the pasta water and drain the rigatoni in a colander.

7. While the pasta is cooking, pour half of the *condimento* into a large serving bowl. Chop the cooled fried eggplant into 1/2-inch pieces and finely chop the sardines. Put half of the chopped eggplant and half of the chopped sardines in the bowl with the *condimento*. Add half of the drained rigatoni to the pasta bowl and mix well. Add the remaining tomato sauce, eggplant, and sardines and enough pasta water to make the pasta slippery. Mix very well. Serve hot with Parmesan cheese on the table.

TIP There needs to be a lot of oil in the pan to fry eggplant, because eggplant drinks a lot of oil. The slices have to be able to swim a little in the oil. It's not true deep-frying, but it's not sautéing, either.

WILD FENNEL

grows in the hills all over Sicily. It has feathery fronds like the tops of regular fennel, but there is no bulb underneath. It is one of the signa-tures of Sicilian cooking, especially for its role in *bucatini con le sarde*, one of our classic dishes and something we like to eat all year. But the season of wild fennel is only a short time in the spring, so before the wild fennel disappears from the mountainsides we harvest as much as we can. We boil it, chop it, drain it, and put it in small plastic bags to freeze and use when we need it. Then we take it out of the freezer and cut off as much as we need. We know that wild fennel grows all over the hillsides in California and that it has a longer season there. If you live where there is wild fennel, I suggest you take advantage of this and freeze it as we do. And if you don't, then the fronds from fennel bulbs will work fine as a substitute in our recipes.

Fusilli with Sausages and Potato
Fusilli con Salsiccia e Patate

Serves 6

Many people are surprised to find potatoes in pasta because it seems they think that with two starches, it's like they are eating pasta and pasta. In fact, the flavors of pasta and potatoes are completely different. We would never, for example, eat bread and pasta together, but in our family, and in much of Sicilian cooking, we love pasta and potatoes together.

1. Put the sausage meat in a big frying pan with the butter, oil, onions, and garlic clove over low heat. Stir together and sauté until the sausages turn golden brown, about 5 minutes. Add a few tablespoons of water if the meat is sticking to the pan. Stir in the cubed potatoes and salt and pepper to taste. Add 1/2 cup of water and cook until the potatoes are tender, adding more water if necessary. Add the tomatoes and cook for about 2 minutes so they break down. Taste again for salt. Stir in the cream and the Parmesan cheese and turn off the heat.

2. Bring a large saucepan of water to a boil over high heat. Stir in a small fistful of salt and the fusilli and cook until the pasta is tender. Save a cupful of pasta water and drain the pasta quickly in a colander. Add the drained fusilli to the pan with the sausage *condimento*. Stir in the hot pepper flakes and the minced parsley and mix with a splash of pasta water over high heat for about 1 minute to reheat the *condimento* with the pasta, adding more pasta water if the pasta is sticky. Transfer to a pasta bowl and serve immediately, with grated Parmesan cheese at the table.

FUSILLI means "corkscrew," and that's exactly what this pasta looks like. It is a substantial pasta, so it needs a rich, flavorful *condimento*. It is also a good shape to use when you are tossing the pasta with something that needs to be stabbed with a fork to pick it up, because the fusilli also needs the fork.

1/2 pound pork sausages, removed from the casings
2 tablespoons unsalted butter
1 tablespoon olive oil
1 small white or yellow onion, chopped
1 garlic clove
2 potatoes, peeled and cut into 1/2-inch cubes
Salt and freshly ground black pepper
2 canned peeled whole tomatoes, drained in a colander and chopped (or 2 Roma tomatoes, peeled and chopped)
1/3 cup heavy cream
2 tablespoons grated Parmesan cheese, plus more for passing at the table
1 pound fusilli
Pinch of hot pepper flakes
1/3 cup finely chopped fresh Italian parsley

TIP When you use just a little bit of canned tomatoes, transfer the leftover tomato into a plastic container. Do not store it in the tin—the tomato will take on the flavor of the can, and it is also bad for the health. Store it in the refrigerator or freezer until ready to use.

Sicily's Famous Spaghetti with Eggplant and Ricotta Salata
Spaghetti alla Norma

Serves 6

"Ricotta salata must be grated directly over the spaghetti, like snow falling on the mountain."
—W.

This spaghetti, named for the famous Sicilian opera Norma, *is a classic. It was first made for the famous composer Vincenzo Bellini to remind him of Mt. Etna, the active volcano located in the western city of Catania, where he's from. It's said that the spaghetti represents the mountain, the eggplant is the lava, and the grated ricotta salata is the snow that caps Etna in the colder months. Etna is the first place on the island to get snow, and the last place the snow melts in the spring.*

Olive oil for deep-frying and
  the pasta water
2 medium eggplants, cut into
  1/2-inch cubes
3 cups Fresh Tomato Sauce (page 9;
  or bottled sauce*)
Salt
1 pound spaghetti
2 tablespoons unsalted butter
1/2 cup (about 2 ounces) grated
  ricotta salata*, plus more for
  passing at the table

*See source list.

1. Pour enough olive oil into a large, deep frying pan to fill it 3 inches deep. Heat the oil until it is very hot but not smoking. (It will sizzle when you drop water in it.) Add the eggplant in batches, being careful not to overcrowd the pan, and fry until it is golden brown on all sides, about 5 minutes. Remove the eggplant with a slotted spoon and place it on a thick bed of paper towels to drain.

2. Slowly heat the tomato sauce in a saucepan over low heat, stirring occasionally to prevent the sauce from sticking to the pot.

3. Meanwhile, bring a large saucepan of water to a boil over high heat. Stir in a small fistful of salt, a splash of olive oil, and the spaghetti. Boil the spaghetti, stirring often to prevent the spaghetti from sticking together, until al dente.

4. Just before the pasta is ready, stir the fried eggplant pieces into the sauce. Put about 1/2 cup of the sauce, 1/2 cup of boiling pasta water, and the butter in the bottom of a pasta bowl.

5. Use a spaghetti strainer to lift the pasta out of the water and into the bowl with the pasta sauce. Add all but a cup of the remaining sauce and toss to coat the spaghetti, adding more hot pasta water if the spaghetti is dry or sticky. Top with the remaining sauce and the grated ricotta salata. Serve immediately, with more grated ricotta salata on the table.

Sicily's Famous Spaghetti with Eggplant and Ricotta Salata

Paolo's Pappardelle with Lamb and Fava Beans Braised in Red Wine
Pappardelle con Fave ed Agnello di Paolo

Serves 4

Paolo loves fava beans, and when they are in season, he finds ways to use them at his inn just about every day. This ragù, *with lamb and red wine, is rich and very delicious.*

1/2 cup extra virgin olive oil, plus more for the pasta water
1 white or yellow onion, chopped
1 pound leg of lamb
Salt and freshly ground black pepper
2 cups dry red wine
4 *rametti* (small stems) of wild fennel

FOR THE FAVAS
1/2 onion, finely chopped
3 garlic cloves, halved
2 1/2 pounds fava beans (in their pods), shelled
Salt and freshly ground black pepper to taste

1/2 pound pappardelle
1/4 cup freshly grated ricotta salata,* plus more for passing at the table

*See source list.

1. Warm 6 tablespoons of the olive oil in a large skillet over medium heat. Add the onion and cook until soft and golden brown, about 15 minutes. Increase heat to high, add the lamb, and sear until it is brown on all sides. Season with salt and pepper to taste. Add 1 cup of the red wine and 2 cups water. Lower the heat and simmer until the onions are very sweet and the lamb is so tender you can take a piece off the bone with no effort, 2 to 2 1/2 hours.

2. Bring a small saucepan of salted water to a boil. Add the fennel and boil until it is tender, about 5 minutes. Drain.

3. To make the favas, start by preparing a *soffritto:* Heat 2 tablespoons of the olive oil over medium heat. Add the onion and sauté until soft. Add the garlic and cook for 2 minutes or until fragrant. Add the fava beans and cook in the *soffritto* until tender. You may need to add some water to keep the fava beans from sticking. Season with salt and pepper to taste. Add the fennel and sauté a few minutes more.

4. Just before you are ready to toss the pasta, warm the lamb and transfer to a strainer to drain the fat. Shred the lamb into a dry skillet. Add the remaining cup of wine and cook over medium-high heat until the lamb is brown and all the wine has evaporated. Transfer the lamb to the pan with the fava beans.

5. Meanwhile, bring a saucepan of water to a boil. Stir in a small fistful of salt and a splash of oil. Add the pappardelle, stir, and cook until al dente. Reserve a cupful of the pasta water and drain the pasta in a colander. Quickly add the pasta and a splash of the pasta water to the pan with the lamb and favas. Toss the pasta with the lamb *condimento* over high heat until they are mixed and warmed through. Add more pasta water if necessary. Transfer to a serving dish and sprinkle with the grated ricotta salata. Serve immediately.

Pasta with Lentil Ragù
Pasta con Ragù di Lenticchie

Serves 6

The combination of lentils and pasta might seem unexpected, but it is very good—a nice, hearty dish for a cold night.

1. Drain the soaked lentils and place them in a big soup pot covered with cool water. Add the quartered potato and salt to taste and bring to a boil over high heat. Reduce the heat and cook at a low boil until the lentils are tender, about 1 1/2 hours. Drain in a colander.

2. To prepare the *soffritto*, heat the oil in a large frying pan over medium heat. Add the onions, carrots, and celery and sauté until the vegetables are tender. Remove from the heat. Stir in the tomato paste, 1/2 cup of water, and the sugar and simmer for 5 minutes. Add the lentils, stir, and adjust the salt, pepper, and sugar to taste. Sauté for about 5 minutes so all the ingredients have a chance to blend.

3. Meanwhile, bring a large saucepan of water to a boil. Add a splash of oil and a small fistful of salt and stir in the torchietti. Boil the pasta until tender. Reserve a cupful of the pasta water and drain the pasta in a colander. Return the pasta to the pan you cooked it in. Place the pan over medium-high heat, pour in the lentil *ragù* and a splash of pasta water, and stir it all together so that the lentils coat the pasta. Cook for 2 to 3 minutes, adding more pasta water if the pasta appears dry. Transfer the pasta to a serving bowl, sprinkle with the grated pecorino, and serve immediately with more grated pecorino on the table.

"When we cook, we must be elastic with our minds. If you don't have celery leaves, use a bit of the stalk instead."

—G.

3/4 pound lentils, soaked overnight
1 large potato, peeled and quartered
Salt
1 cup extra virgin olive oil, plus more for the pasta water
1 small white or yellow onion, chopped
2 medium carrots, chopped
A small handful (4–6) celery leaves, finely chopped
2 tablespoons tomato paste
1 teaspoon sugar (or more to taste)
Freshly ground black pepper
1 pound torchietti
2 tablespoons freshly grated pecorino cheese, plus more for passing at the table

TORCHIETTI
means "little press." This shape of pasta is a short hollow tube with ridges and a slight twist to it, like a small screw. If you don't have torchietti, you can use gnocchetti instead.

Bucatini with Sausages, Pecorino, and Cinnamon
Bucatini con Salsiccia e Pecorino alla Madonita

Serves 4

Sausage and pecorino are like brothers here in the mountains of Sicily; the two just go together. When you hear "sausages and pecorino," you can immediately smell the flavor of the countryside. In Gangi, we ask the butcher to make our sausages with fennel seeds. If you can't get fennel sausages where you are, add a pinch of seeds to the pan when you're sautéing the sausage.

1/2 pound Italian sausage,
  removed from casings
1 cup milk
Salt
3/4 pound bucatini
1/2 pound fresh ricotta*
Pinch of cinnamon
Freshly ground black pepper
1/4 cup grated pecorino cheese, plus
  more for passing at the table

See source list.

TIP When you're browning the meat and you need to add water to the pan, add it a little at a time. You want the meat to be a nice rich brown. If you add all the water at once, you wash the meat.

1. Heat a nonstick frying pan over medium heat. Add the sausage meat and fry for 1 to 2 minutes, breaking the meat into small pieces as it cooks, until it begins to brown. (If you find the sausage meat sticking to the pan, add a splash of water.) Gradually add the milk and continue to cook on medium heat until the mixture has a creamy texture, about 5 minutes.

2. Bring a large saucepan of water to a boil. Stir in a small fistful of salt and the pasta and cook until the pasta is tender. Save a cupful of the pasta water and drain the pasta in a colander.

3. While the pasta is cooking, place the ricotta in a medium bowl. Add the cinnamon and salt and pepper to taste and work it together with a fork until the ricotta is smooth. Add a splash of the hot pasta water if necessary to make the ricotta creamy.

4. Quickly transfer the cooked pasta and 1/2 cup of the pasta water to the frying pan with the sausages and stir over medium–high heat to combine. Stir in the ricotta, grated pecorino, and a splash of pasta water and cook for 1 minute to warm through. Add more pasta water if the *condimento* appears dry or sticky. Transfer to a serving bowl and pass grated pecorino at the table.

Little Penne with Potatoes and Eggs
Pennette con Patate e Uova

Serves 4

In the last couple of years, we in the countryside in Sicily have discovered the pleasure of planting our own potatoes. It turns out to be like a sort of game, like discovering a treasure: golden stones in the earth. Because when you harvest potatoes, you pull 1 plant and—boom!—there are 8 or 10 potatoes there! It's important to use freshly grated pepper in this recipe, because both the potatoes and the eggs need that extra scent of the fresh pepper to bring out their flavor.

1. Warm 1 1/2 cups of the olive oil and the walnut of butter together in a big saucepan over high heat until it is hot but not smoking. Spread the potatoes out in the pan in an even layer and season with salt and pepper to taste. Sauté the potatoes without turning them, until the undersides are golden brown. Then turn them over with a slotted spoon or spatula to cook the other side until golden.

2. Bring a big saucepan of water to a boil. Add a fistful of salt and the pennette and cook, stirring often, until the pasta is tender. Reserve a cupful of the pasta water and drain the pasta in a colander.

3. While the pasta is cooking, crack the eggs into a small bowl. Add the grated pecorino and a pinch of salt and beat together with a fork.

4. Pour the remaining 1/4 cup of olive oil into a large frying pan over high heat. When the oil is warm, add the drained pasta. Pour the beaten eggs over the pasta and mix the eggs and pasta together with a spatula or wooden spoon. Add the potatoes while the eggs are still runny. Sprinkle with freshly ground black pepper, mix again, and cook until the eggs are done. Transfer to a serving bowl and serve immediately with grated pecorino on the table.

Penne means "quill," so **PENNETTE** means "small quills," which is what they are—small penne. *Mezze penne,* incidentally, are "half quills." If you can't find pennette, penne will work fine in its place.

1 3/4 cups extra virgin olive oil
A walnut of butter (about 2 tablespoons)
3/4 pound potatoes, peeled and cut into cubes
Salt and freshly ground black pepper
1 pound pennette
6 large eggs
1/3 cup (about 1 ounce) freshly grated pecorino cheese, plus more for the table

"Don't stir all the time. I always say the food in the pan doesn't want to be disturbed."

—G.

"My father couldn't stand salt cod and we were not allowed to have it in the house until he was no longer with us. My mother loves it. By soaking the salt cod in the water a long time, it loses its wild fishy smell and also mellows out its taste."

—G.

1/2 pound boned salt cod
1 cup extra virgin olive oil
3 scallions, thinly sliced (white part only)
1 small hot red pepper, seeded and minced
1 fresh bay leaf
Pinch of dried oregano
Salt
3/4 cup finely chopped fresh Italian parsley, plus extra for garnish
2 whole garlic cloves
1 pound broccoli rabe, trimmed and coarsely chopped
5 anchovy fillets in oil, chopped
1 pound tubetti rigati
Freshly grated Parmesan cheese

TUBETTI RIGATI
are "little tubes with ridges." If you cannot find them, penne, mezze penne, or pennette rigate will all work fine.

Tubetti with Salt Cod and Broccoli Rabe
Tubetti con Baccalà e Cime di Rapa

Serves 6

This recipe came from a woman in Gangi. We met her when she was buying the salt cod to make this dish. She was arguing with the seller about price and screaming so loudly that the poor man had to discount the fish before everybody ran away from his shop. In the end, the woman, embarrassed and smiling, offered to give the customers her recipe for pasta and baccalà as compensation. So here it is.

1. Place the salt cod in a pot and cover with cool water. Soak the cod for at least 12 hours, changing the water every few hours. (If you want to soak it overnight, it's enough to change the water once before you go to bed and once again in the morning.) Remove the cod from the water and break it up with your fingers to remove any small bones that remain.

2. Heat half of the olive oil in a saucepan over medium–high heat. Add the scallions and sauté for about 3 minutes, until they are soft and beginning to have color. Add the small pieces of salt cod to the pan. Stir in the hot pepper, bay leaf, oregano, and salt to taste. (Be careful with the salt, as the cod is very salty.) Cover the pan and cook for 5 minutes, until the fish has a little color. Add a splash of water to the pan if it appears dry or if the cod is sticking to the bottom. Add 1/4 cup of the parsley, mix well, and turn off the heat.

3. Heat the remaining olive oil in a large frying pan over medium heat. Add the garlic cloves and sauté until they are light golden. Remove the garlic cloves, add the chopped broccoli rabe and 1/2 cup of water, and sauté for about 10 minutes, until the greens are very tender. Add the chopped anchovy fillets, 1/2 cup of the parsley, and salt to taste and mix well. Turn off the heat.

4. Bring a large saucepan of water to a boil. Stir in a small fistful of salt and the tubetti and cook until the pasta is tender. Save a cupful of the pasta water and drain the pasta quickly in a colander. Return the pasta to the pan you cooked it in. Add the cod and the broccoli rabe and mix them with the pasta over high heat for about 1 minute. Transfer to a pasta bowl, sprinkle with the remaining parsley, and serve immediately. Pass the Parmesan.

Spaghetti with Clams and Mushrooms
Spaghetti con Vongole e Funghi

Serves 4

This pasta is like a romantic meeting of land and sea: in this case, the funghi of our rustic, rugged countryside, and the clams from our deep Sicilian blue sea. Whenever we order clams in a restaurant, we always ask the waiter, "vongole veraci?" which means, "Are the clams really fresh?" To us, fresh means from the sea that day. When he answers, we look closely into his eyes to see if he is telling the truth. When we make this pasta, it is always when we have brought the mushrooms from Gangivecchio to Palermo, not the clams from Palermo to Gangivecchio. It would seem strange to us and to our guests to eat clams in the country, because they would not seem really fresh.

1. Wash the octopus, cut off the skin, and cut into 1/2-inch pieces. Clean the mushrooms and cut them into 1/2-inch slices.

2. Put the clams with 1 cup of water in a large saucepan over high heat. Bring to a boil and simmer until the shells open. Drain the clams and set aside, reserving the water.

3. Place the oil and garlic in the saucepan you cooked the clams in over medium heat and sauté until the garlic is light golden brown. Discard the garlic and add the octopus, mushroom slices, tomatoes, and reserved clam water. Season with salt to taste, cover, and simmer for 15 minutes. Uncover and cook for another 10 minutes on low heat until the mushrooms are very tender, adding more water if the pan gets dry.

4. Meanwhile, bring a large saucepan of water to a boil. Stir in a small fistful of salt and a splash of olive oil. Add the spaghetti, stir to prevent it from sticking together, and boil until the spaghetti is al dente. Lift the spaghetti out of the water with a spaghetti strainer and place it directly into the pan with the octopus and mushrooms. Add the clams, 1/4 cup of the basil, 1/4 cup of the parsley, and salt and pepper to taste, and mix very well over high heat for 1 or 2 minutes to warm through. Transfer to a serving dish, sprinkle with the remaining basil and parsley, and serve immediately.

3/4 pound small octopus
1 pound (uncooked) portobello mushrooms, coarsely chopped
10 ounces clams in the shells, soaked in salted water for 1 hour
1/2 cup olive oil, plus more for the pasta water
1 garlic clove
10 ounces fresh tomatoes, peeled, seeded, and cubed
Salt
3/4 pound spaghetti
1/2 cup finely chopped fresh basil
1/2 cup finely chopped fresh Italian parsley
Freshly ground black pepper

Fusilli with Fresh Shell Beans
Fusilli con Fagioli Freschi

Serves 6

We always fight with Peppe to plant fresh shell beans in our home garden. We love shell beans, but Peppe is reluctant to plant them because he knows he'll be the one to shell them. Last year, we found the solution. We had Mariano plant them, because Mario does whatever he's asked. We grew lots of shell beans, which were the inspiration for this recipe.

1/2 cup extra virgin olive oil
1 carrot, finely chopped
1 celery stalk, thinly sliced
1 small white or yellow onion, diced
1/4 pound pancetta (or bacon), cut into 1/2–inch cubes
1 garlic clove, minced
1 pound fresh tomatoes, peeled, seeded, and cubed
1 pound fresh beans (such as borlotti beans), shelled
4 cups vegetable broth
Salt and freshly ground black pepper
1/3 cup finely chopped fresh Italian parsley
1 pound fusilli
A walnut of butter (about 2 table-spoons)
1/4 cup freshly grated pecorino cheese, plus more for the table

1. Warm the olive oil in a large frying pan over low heat. Add the carrot, celery, onion, and pancetta and sauté for 3 to 4 minutes, until the onions begin to soften. Add the garlic, tomatoes, and beans and sauté, stirring often, for about 5 minutes, being careful not to let the garlic brown. Add the vegetable broth and salt and pepper to taste. Cover and simmer the beans with the vegetables over low heat until the beans are very tender but not falling apart, about 30 minutes. Turn off the heat and stir in the parsley.

2. Bring a large saucepan of water to a boil. Stir in a small fistful of salt and the fusilli and cook until the pasta is tender. Reserve a cupful of the pasta water and drain the pasta in a colander. Add the fusilli to the pan with the beans and place over high heat. Stir in the butter and enough pasta water to make the pasta moist and slippery and mix well. Transfer to a pasta bowl and sprinkle with the pecorino cheese. Serve immediately, with more grated pecorino on the table.

TIP You must taste beans to know if they're done. You want to make sure they're cooked enough so that they have a nice, creamy texture. If the skin is hard when you bite into one, you need to cook it longer.

Bucatini with Dried Figs
Bucatini con Fichi Secchi

Serves 6

I love figs, both fresh and dried. Since my brother already makes the ultimate pasta using fresh figs, it was my fantasy to invent a pasta using the dried version. Before inventing this recipe, I tried another; it was so unsuccessful, even our pasta-loving dogs wouldn't eat it. But I was still convinced that dried figs should make a wonderful condimento for a pasta, so I played around until I got this. We have a big fig tree in the courtyard at Gangivecchio that gives many figs, but we eat them fresh because it is a boring and tedious task to dry them. We buy the dried figs for this recipe at the market in Palermo. —G.

1. Put the butter in a large saucepan. Drain the onions, add them to the saucepan, and sauté over low heat for about 5 minutes, until they are tender and golden. Pour the wine over the onions and simmer for about 20 minutes or until the onions are almost melted. Add a splash of hot water if the onions are sticking to the pan. Turn off the heat and season with salt and pepper to taste.

2. Bring a big saucepan of water to a boil. Stir in a small fistful of salt and a splash of oil. Add the bucatini and cook until tender. Reserve a cupful of the pasta water and drain the bucatini through a colander.

3. Quickly transfer the bucatini to the pan with the simmered onions and place over medium–high heat. Add the figs, almonds, and hot pepper and mix all the ingredients together for about 2 minutes to warm. Transfer the pasta to a serving bowl. Top with grated provola cheese and serve immediately, with more grated cheese on the table.

TIP Soaking onions makes them sweeter and softer. Since the figs are sweet, we want the onion taste to be subtle.

4 tablespoons (1/2 stick) unsalted butter

1 pound white or yellow onions, thinly sliced and soaked in cool water for 30 minutes

1/2 cup dry white wine

Salt and freshly ground black pepper

Soybean oil (or other mild–flavored oil) for the pasta water

1 pound bucatini

3 ounces dried figs, soaked in tepid water for at least 2 hours and chopped

1/2 cup peeled almonds, toasted and chopped

1/2 teaspoon hot pepper flakes or cayenne

1/4 pound (about 1 cup) smoked provola cheese grated, plus more for the table

Farfalle with Artichoke Hearts, Fava Beans, and Peas
Farfalle con Carciofi, Fave e Piselli

Serves 6

Known as "la frittella," this is a classic mixture of the Sicilian kitchen: artichoke hearts, fava beans, and peas, all sautéd until they are tender and delicious. It was very much appreciated by Prince Charles when he once came to Gangivecchio for lunch, in 1990. We took this combination and tossed it with pasta, which is not so traditional but is just as tasty.

3 pounds fresh fava beans, shelled (about 1 1/2 cups shelled beans)
1 cup extra virgin olive oil
1 medium white or yellow onion, 1/2 sliced, 1/2 left whole
Salt and freshly ground black pepper
3 small (not miniature) artichokes
1 garlic clove
1/2 pound frozen or fresh shelled green peas
4 tablespoons (1/2 stick) unsalted butter
1 pound farfalle
1/3 cup finely chopped fresh Italian parsley
Freshly grated Parmesan cheese

1. Put the fava beans in a large skillet with 1/2 cup of the olive oil, the sliced onions, and salt and pepper to taste. Cook the favas over low heat until they are tender, 30 to 40 minutes, adding water to the pan from time to time if necessary to prevent the vegetables from sticking.

2. While the favas are cooking, cut the pointed end of each artichoke so it is squared off. Remove the outer leaves. On older artichokes, there will be what we call a "beard"–you call it a "choke." Carve this out and discard. Quarter the artichokes and put them in a large skillet with the remaining 1/2 cup olive oil, the garlic, and salt and pepper to taste and cook over low heat until tender, about 20 minutes, again adding water to the pan as necessary.

3. In a third large skillet, cook the peas with the butter and the whole half onion until tender, about 10 minutes. Season with salt and pepper to taste.

4. Discard the onion half and mix the cooked vegetables together in one of the skillets.

5. Meanwhile, bring a large saucepan of water to boil. Stir in a small fistful of salt and the farfalle and boil the pasta until tender. Save a cupful of the pasta water and drain quickly in a colander. Return the pasta to the pan you cooked it in, stir in the vegetables and a splash of pasta water, and sauté over medium heat to warm the vegetables and mix them with the pasta. Sprinkle with the parsley and Parmesan cheese and serve immediately, with more grated Parmesan on the table.

Our artichokes are smaller than yours. We recommend you use young, small artichokes if you can find them.

Tagliatelle with Meat Gravy and Porcini Mushrooms
Tagliatelle con Sugo di Arrosto e Porcini

Serves 6

This is a very rich dish—both in terms of flavor and of the cost of the veal, porcini, and fresh pasta it is made with. If you can find fresh porcini, of course use them in place of dried. For this pasta, you cook the veal just to have the estratto di carne, *the broth. After the meat is cooked, you can break it into pieces and use it for another pasta or eat it at room temperature with bread.*

1. Pour enough flour on a plate to cover and dredge the veal.

2. Melt the butter with a spoonful of water in a large saucepan over low heat. Add the onions and sweat until tender, 10 to 15 minutes. Increase the heat to medium-high. Add the meat and sear it on all sides to a rich brown color. Add the wine and cook about 3 minutes, until the alcohol smell evaporates. Add the broth, bring to a simmer, and cook the veal on low heat for 1 hour, adding more water if necessary. Add salt and pepper to taste. Add the cream and cook until the liquid is creamy. Remove the meat, save for another use, and reserve the sauce.

3. Heat the olive oil in a large frying pan over low heat. Add the porcini, parsley, and salt and pepper to taste and cook for about 10 minutes until the porcini are tender. Add the porcini and pan juices to the veal sauce.

4. Meanwhile, bring a large saucepan of water to a boil. Stir in a small fistful of salt and a splash of olive oil. Add the tagliatelle and cook until al dente. Reserve a cupful of pasta water and drain the pasta quickly. Put half of the pasta in a serving bowl, add half of the sauce, a splash of pasta water, and half of the grated pecorino, and mix well. Add the remaining pasta, the remaining sauce, and the remaining pecorino and mix again, adding pasta water if the pasta is dry. Transfer to a serving dish and serve immediately, with more grated pecorino on the table.

All-purpose flour for dredging
  the veal
One 1 1/4-pound veal roast
4 tablespoons (1/2 stick) unsalted
  butter
1 small white or yellow onion,
  chopped
1 cup dry white wine
4 cups veal or beef broth
Salt and freshly ground black pepper
1/2 cup heavy cream
1/2 cup extra virgin olive oil, plus
  more for the pasta water
1 cup dried porcini mushrooms,
  soaked in hot water for at least 20
  minutes and sliced
1/3 cup finely chopped fresh Italian
  parsley
1 pound fresh egg tagliatelle
1/2 cup (about 1 1/2 ounces) freshly
  grated pecorino cheese, plus
  more to pass at the table

Ditali with Cauliflower and Cinnamon
Ditali con Broccoli e Cannella

The cauliflower and cinnamon in this simple pasta are two very Sicilian ingredients. We don't normally put them together, but they make this simple pasta something extraordinary.

Salt
1 medium cauliflower, cut into
  bite–size florets
2 garlic cloves
1/2 cup fresh Italian parsley leaves
1 1/2 cups extra virgin olive oil
2 small hot red peppers
2 teaspoons ground cinnamon
1 pound ditali
1/3 cup (about 1 ounce) freshly grated
  pecorino cheese, plus more to pass
  at the table

1. Bring a big saucepan of water to a boil. Stir in a small fistful of salt and add the cauliflower. Boil the cauliflower until al dente, 3 to 5 minutes. Lift it out with a strainer and save the water.

2. Mince the garlic and parsley together. Heat the oil in a big saucepan over low heat. Add the parsley and garlic and the hot peppers and cook for about 5 minutes, until the garlic is fragrant and the pepper soft. Add the cauliflower, sprinkle with the cinnamon, and season with salt and pepper. Sauté for about 2 minutes, stirring often to integrate the flavors. Remove and discard the peppers.

3. Add enough water to the water you cooked the cauliflower in to cook the pasta. Bring it to a boil. Stir in more salt to taste and the ditali and cook until the pasta is tender. Drain the pasta quickly, reserving a cup of the pasta water, and add pasta to the pan with the sauce. Sprinkle with the grated pecorino, add a splash of pasta water, and stir together over high heat for 1 minute. Add more pasta water if necessary to make the pasta slippery and moist. Transfer to a serving bowl and serve immediately, with more grated pecorino on the table.

We use cauliflower in many pasta dishes, including one of our classics, Pasta alla Palina.

Bucatini with Sardines, Fennel, Pine Nuts, and Currants
Bucatini con le Sarde

Serves 6

This is a classic of the Sicilian kitchen. Every person in Sicily has his or her own recipe for bucatini con le sarde. *Even though the differences are subtle, because the basic ingredients—sardines, wild fennel, currants, pine nuts, and bucatini—are always the same, everyone is convinced that his or her recipe is the best.* Bucatini con le sarde *is one of the very few pastas that we toss with the* condimento *and let sit before serving. We say it needs to rest. We usually give it about 10 minutes, but you can toss it in the morning to eat later that day if you like. If you do this, add oil and water to the pan and reheat it over medium heat.*

"Breaking bucatini in half makes it somewhat manageable to eat."
—G.

1. Place the fennel in a medium saucepan of salted water and bring to a boil over high heat. Reduce the heat and cook the fennel at a low boil until it is very tender, about 10 minutes. Remove the fennel with a slotted spoon and transfer it to a cutting board, reserving the fennel water for cooking the pasta. When it is cool enough to touch, finely chop the fennel bulbs and fronds.

2. Warm 1 cup of the oil in a large saucepan over medium heat. Add the onion and sauté until it is tender and just golden, about 5 minutes. Add the anchovies and sauté until they have dissolved. Add the sardines and salt and pepper to taste and sauté for about 5 minutes, until the sardines begin to fall apart. Stir in the currants, pine nuts, and fennel and sauté for another 5 minutes. For this pasta, the ingredients must be swimming in oil, so if they are not, add more oil and sauté a bit longer—otherwise the dish will turn out very dry. Turn off the heat and let the *condimento* rest while you boil the pasta.

3. Add enough water to the reserved fennel water to cook the pasta and bring to a boil over high heat. Stir in the saffron and salt to taste. Add the broken pasta along with a splash of olive oil and cook, stirring often, until the pasta is tender.

4. Remove a cupful of the pasta water and drain the pasta in a colander. Don't worry if the tubes hold some of the pasta water. The *condimento* will need the water to thin it a bit. Return the pasta to the pot you cooked it in. Add two-thirds of the *condimento*, the remaining 1/4 cup of olive oil, and a splash of pasta water, and toss gently. Cover the pot and let the pasta rest, off the heat, for about 10 minutes. Before serving, toss

2 medium fennel bulbs and their greens, or the equivalent of wild fennel

1 1/4 cup extra virgin olive oil (or more if necessary), plus a little extra for the pasta water

1 large white or yellow onion, finely chopped

6 anchovy fillets in oil

2 1/2 pounds cleaned whole fresh or frozen sardines, rinsed and drained in a colander

Salt and freshly ground black pepper

1/2 cup currants, soaked in tepid water for 10 minutes and drained

1/2 cup pine nuts

1 pound bucatini, broken in half

A pinch of ground saffron or saffron threads

Toasted breadcrumbs for passing at the table

CLEANING SARDINES is not something we would ever do at home. It is very tedious and specialized work, something for the fishmonger to take care of. What it means is that each tiny fish has been scaled, washed, boned, finned, and deheaded. Two and a half pounds of whole sardines will yield about 1 pound of cleaned sardines. Once we get the sardines home, we rinse them under cold water and pat them dry with paper towels.

the pasta again and transfer to a warm serving bowl. Top with the extra *condimento* and a sprinkling of toasted breadcrumbs. Serve with more toasted breadcrumbs on the table.

TIP We always stir at the same time that we add the pasta to the water. The pasta wants attention. It doesn't want to be dumped in the water and then left to cook by itself. Stir it from time to time to keep it happy and so that it doesn't stick. Being nearby will also keep you from over–cooking the pasta accidentally.

Straight from the sea

Bucatini with Cauliflower, Currants, and Pine Nuts
Bucatini alla Palina

Serves 6

TIP For us, "lightly salted water" means at least a tablespoon of salt. You have to add enough to the water to be able to taste it.

Palina is the name of an order of monks in Sicily that supposedly invented this dish. The combination of cauliflower, currants, and pine nuts might sound strange if you are not Sicilian and if you have not tried it, but it really is delicious. This, like pasta con le sarde, is a dish you don't serve immediately after it's tossed with the condimento. It's best if you let it sit for 5 to 10 minutes, covered, after tossing it. If the pasta seems sticky after it has rested, add a little hot pasta water to make it creamier.

1. Bring a large saucepan of lightly salted water to a boil. Add the cauliflower florets and cook for 3 to 4 minutes, until the cauliflower is just tender. Use a slotted spoon to remove the cauliflower from the water. Reserve the water for the *condimento* and to cook the pasta.

2. Heat the olive oil in a saucepan over medium heat. Add the shallots and anchovies and sauté until the anchovies have dissolved and the shallots are tender and slightly golden, about 5 minutes. Add the cauliflower, saffron, currants, pine nuts, and 1/2 cup of the cauliflower water and cook over low heat for 15 to 20 minutes, until all the ingredients are melded together and creamy. If the pan gets dry, add some more cauliflower water as you go.

3. Meanwhile, combine 1 quart of cauliflower water with about 3 quarts of water in a large saucepan and bring it to a boil over high heat. Stir in a small fistful of salt and a splash of olive oil. Add the broken bucatini and cook until tender, stirring often. Reserve a cupful of the pasta water and drain the bucatini in a colander.

4. Return the bucatini to the pot you cooked it in. Add the cauliflower *condimento* and a splash of the pasta water and toss to coat the pasta. Add more pasta water if the pasta is at all dry or sticky. Cover the pot and let the pasta rest, off the heat, for 5 minutes. Before serving, toss the pasta again, transfer it to a serving bowl, and top with a sprinkling of toasted breadcrumbs. Pass a bowl of toasted breadcrumbs as you would grated cheese at the table.

Salt
1 small cauliflower, cut into small florets
3/4 cup extra virgin olive oil, plus more for the pasta water
4 shallots (or 1/2 medium white or yellow onion), finely chopped
3 anchovy fillets in oil
1/4 teaspoon saffron threads or powder
1/2 cup currants, soaked in tepid water for 10 minutes and drained
1/4 cup pine nuts
1 pound bucatini, broken in half
Toasted breadcrumbs for passing at the table

TIP We always boil our vegetables. We know that Americans prefer to steam them. If it makes you feel better, you can steam vegetables like the cauliflower for this pasta. But try to use a lot of steaming water and remember to save that water. We often use it to cook the pasta. We think it makes a subtle but important difference—to integrate the flavor of the vegetables into the pasta itself.

Orietta's Linguine with Shrimp and Fried Artichokes
Linguine con Gamberi e Carciofi Fritti di Orietta

Serves 6

Our friend Orietta made this for us at her home. We liked it so much, we asked if we could include it in our book.

2 medium artichokes
Juice of 1 lemon
All-purpose flour for coating the artichokes
1/3 cup extra virgin olive oil, plus more for frying the artichokes and for the pasta water
Salt
2 pounds small shrimp, shelled and deveined
1 cup dry white wine
1 pound linguine
1/4 cup finely chopped fresh Italian parsley

1. Trim the stem ends and cut the tops off the artichokes so they are squared off. Remove the tough outer leaves, cut out the chokes, and cut the artichokes into eighths. Soak the artichokes in a bowl with water to cover and the lemon juice. When you're ready to fry the artichokes, drain and pat them dry with paper towels.

2. Put some flour in a bowl and dredge the artichokes. Pour enough olive oil in a saucepan to fill to 1 1/2 inches deep. Heat the oil to very hot but not smoking over medium-high heat. Add the artichokes and fry, turning them occasionally, until they are golden on all sides. Remove the artichokes from the oil with a slotted spoon and drain on a bed of paper towels. Cover the artichokes with a dishcloth or place them in a warm oven to keep them warm.

3. Bring a medium saucepan of salted water to a boil over high heat. Add the shrimp and boil for about 5 minutes, until the shrimp are pink and cooked through. Drain in a colander.

4. Pour the wine and the 1/3 cup of olive oil into the pan you cooked the shrimp in and warm them over medium heat for 3 to 5 minutes, or until the liquid reduces by one-third.

5. Bring a large saucepan of water to a boil. Stir in a small fistful of salt and a splash of olive oil. Stir in the linguine and cook until the pasta is al dente, stirring often to prevent it from sticking together. In the meantime, reheat the wine-oil mixture. Remove the pasta from the water using a spaghetti strainer, and transfer it to a serving bowl. Pour the warm wine-oil mixture, the boiled shrimp, the fried artichokes, and a ladleful of the hot pasta water into the bowl with the pasta. Toss well to mix the ingredients together, adding more hot pasta water if the linguine looks dry. Sprinkle with the parsley and serve immediately.

Lasagne Ricce with Fresh Sausages
Lasagne Ricce con Ragù di Salsiccia

Serves 6

The combination of sausages and estratto *make this a very rich-tasting pasta.*

TIP You must be very careful when you melt *estratto*, which is Sicily's sun-dried-tomato paste, in the oil. Put the heat on low, and break the paste up with a wooden spoon. When it starts to bubble up, add a little water. If the heat is too high, the *estratto* will become lumpy.

1. Heat the oil and the *estratto* together in a large saucepan over medium heat. Add 1 cup of hot water (less if you're using tomato paste), stirring constantly until the *estratto* has melted. Add the sausage, celery, onion, sugar, and enough water to just cover the ingredients and stir. Season with salt and pepper to taste. Bring to a boil, then reduce the heat to low and simmer for 1 hour, until the vegetables are tender and the ingredients are mixed together. Taste for seasoning and add more salt, pepper, and sugar to taste.

2. Meanwhile, bring a large saucepan of water to a boil. Stir in a small fistful of salt, a splash of oil, and the pasta. Cook until the pasta is tender. When the pasta is almost cooked, spoon a ladleful of the hot *condimento* into a serving bowl. Reserve a cupful of the pasta water, drain the pasta quickly in a colander, and put it into the bowl with the *condimento*. Add the rest of the *condimento* and a splash of pasta water, and toss the pasta well, adding some pasta water if it is dry or sticky. Top with a sprinkling of freshly grated pecorino cheese and pass more at the table. Serve immediately.

1/3 cup extra virgin olive oil, plus
   more for the pasta water
1 cup *estratto** (or tomato paste)
1 1/2 pounds sweet Italian sausage,
   cut into 1-inch rounds
2 stalks celery, diced
1 small white or yellow onion, diced
1 teaspoon sugar (or more to taste)
Salt and freshly ground black pepper
1 pound lasagne ricce
Freshly grated pecorino cheese

See source list.

One-Dish Pastas
(Piatti Unici)

66. Festonate with Pancetta, Peppers, and Portobello Mushrooms Surrounded by Port–Braised Chicken Drumsticks
    (*Festonate con Pollo e Porto*)

67. Papa's Ricotta Ravioli with Simple Butter Sauce
    (*Ravioli di Ricotta di Papà*)

    Variation: Fish Ravioli with Sweet Pepper Sauce
    (*Ravioli di Merluzzo o Cernia con Salsa di Peperoni*)

    Variation: Ravioli with Ricotta, Potatoes, and Pancetta
    (*Ravioli di Ricotta, Patate e Pancetta*)

68. Orecchiette with Lobster and Prosecco
    (*Orecchiette con Aragosta*)

69. Glutton's Tortiglioni
    (*I Tortiglioni del Goloso*)

70. Maccheroncini with Marsala, Chicken, and Prosciutto Cotto "For Hunters" (*I Maccheroncini del Cacciatore*)

71. Ziti with Lamb, Lemon, and Rosemary
    (*Ziti al Profumi d'Agnello*)

72. Mixed Seafood with Egg Fettuccine
   (Fettuccine all'Uovo con Pesce)

73. Mezze Penne Rigate with Pork Ragù and Swiss Chard
   (Mezze Penne Rigate con Ragù di Maiale e Giri)

74. Spaghetti with Sea Urchin
   (Spaghetti con Ricci di Mondello)

75. Mondello-Style Spaghetti with Lobster
   (Spaghetti con L'Aragosta)

76. Tagliatelle with Dried Fava Beans and Leafy Green Vegetables
   (Tagliatelle con Fave Secche e Verdure)

77. Ditaloni with Eggplant Balls, Potato, and Pancetta
   (Ditaloni con Polpettine di Melanzane, Patate e Pancetta)

78. Spaghetti with Veal Bolognese
   (Spaghetti con Ragù di Tritato)

79. Rigatoni with Meat, Eggplant, and Peas in Tomato Sauce
   (La Pasta dei Monaci)

We always call the pasta, risotto, or soup the "primo piatto." The meat or fish we follow it with is the "secondo." We call a dish with the meat and the pasta on the same plate "piatto unico," "single dish," because it is so substantial that you don't need another. We Italians are used to having two courses, so even with a piatto unico, we might still serve a salad or a plate of cheeses after, just for the ritual of it.

Festonate with Pancetta, Peppers, and Portobello Mushrooms Surrounded by Port-Braised Chicken Drumsticks

Festonate with Pancetta, Peppers, and Portobello Mushrooms Surrounded by Port–Braised Chicken Drumsticks
Festonate con Pollo e Porto

Serves 6

We Sicilians prefer dark-meat chicken to white meat. We know that in the United States, many people prefer the breasts. When we buy whole chickens, we often boil the breasts and feed them to our beloved cats and dogs, because in most cases, we think they are too dry and without enough flavor for most dishes. For this dish, we like to use drumsticks because they look very festive around the platter.

6 chicken legs (drumsticks)
1/2 cup all–purpose flour
Salt and freshly ground black pepper
1/4 cup extra virgin olive oil, plus more for frying chicken and for the pasta water
12 tablespoons (1 1/2 sticks) unsalted butter
1/2 pound pancetta (or bacon), cut into 1/2–inch cubes
6 scallions (white part only), thinly sliced
3/4 pound red and yellow bell peppers, cored, seeded, and diced
1/2 pound portobello mushrooms, cut into 1/2–inch cubes
One 28–ounce can peeled whole tomatoes, drained in a colander and broken into pieces
1 tablespoon sugar (or more to taste)
Pinch of cayenne pepper or hot pepper flakes
1 cup port wine
4 sprigs fresh thyme
1 pound festonate
Freshly grated Parmesan cheese

1. Remove the skin from the chicken legs. Pour the flour on a plate and season it with salt and pepper. Roll the chicken legs through the seasoned flour so they are evenly coated.

2. Pour enough oil into a large frying pan to fill to 3/4 inch deep. Add the butter and heat until it is melted. Turn the heat to high, add the chicken legs, and fry, turning them occasionally, until they're cooked through and golden brown on all sides, about 5 minutes. Remove the chicken from the frying pan and place on a plate lined with paper towels while you prepare the sauce. Discard the oil and butter you fried the chicken in.

3. Warm 1/4 cup of olive oil in a large frying pan over medium heat. Add the pancetta and sauté for about 5 minutes, until the pancetta is golden brown and slightly crispy. Add the scallions and peppers and sauté for about 5 minutes more, until the peppers are soft. Add the mushrooms and a splash of water to the pan to keep the vegetables from sticking. Salt the mushrooms and sauté them over medium heat for about 5 minutes, adding more water if the pan is dry, until the mushrooms are tender but not mushy.

"The minute you add tomatoes, all the other vegetables in the pan will stop cooking. So always add the tomatoes after the vegetables are golden brown."

—W.

4. Add the tomatoes. Sprinkle the tomatoes with the sugar, hot pepper, and salt and simmer for a few minutes, until tomatoes begin to break down.

5. Place the cooked chicken legs in the frying pan with the tomatoes. Pour the port over the chicken and cook until the alcohol has evaporated. Add the fresh thyme sprigs and a cup of water. Cover the pan and cook the chicken with the *condimento* for 20 minutes over low heat. Check on this from time to time to see if you need to add water, and taste to see if you want more sugar or salt.

6. Bring a big saucepan of water to a boil. Stir in a small fistful of salt, a splash of olive oil, and the festonate and boil, stirring occasionally, until the pasta is tender. Reserve some pasta water and drain the festonate quickly through a colander.

7. Add the festonate to the skillet with the *condimento*. Mix the pasta with the *condimento* over high heat for a few minutes, adding some pasta water if the pasta is too dry. Transfer the pasta to a large serving platter. Place the chicken legs around the platter, and serve hot with grated Parmesan cheese.

"My mother adds sugar everywhere. I think chicken is the only thing she doesn't add sugar to."
—G.

"It's always tasty to sprinkle tomatoes with a little bit of sugar."
—W.

Papa's Ricotta Ravioli with Simple Butter Sauce
Ravioli di Ricotta di Papà

Serves 8

My mamma got this recipe more than 50 years ago on a trip to Taormina with my father. There was a woman cooking in a restaurant there who was Austrian. My father was so fond of the ravioli that my mother asked the woman for the recipe. She has continually made these ravioli for special dinners during all these years. —G.

All-purpose flour for dusting
3 pounds fresh ricotta,* drained
  in a fine-mesh colander
Pinch of salt
1 recipe for Fresh Pasta Dough
  (page 8)
5 cups chicken broth
10 tablespoons (1 1/4 sticks) unsalted
  butter
2/3 cup (about 2 ounces) grated
  Parmesan cheese, plus more
  for the table

See source list.

1. Line 2 large sheet pans with clean dishtowels. Dust the towels with flour and set aside until you are ready to cut the ravioli.
2. Place the drained ricotta in a large bowl. Mash it up with a fork. Add the salt and mash it some more. Taste for salt and add more if necessary.
3. Roll out the fresh pasta dough into a rectangular shape, about 18 inches long by 5 inches wide, and 1/8 inch thick. Place the dough so that the long side is facing you.
4. Place a rounded teaspoonful of ricotta 3 inches from the lengthwise edge of the dough. Continue across the length of the rolled-out dough, leaving about 1 1/2 inches between each mound of ricotta. When you've come to the end of the dough, pick the pasta up by the edge closest to you and fold it over so the seam is facing away from you. You'll have to do this a little bit at a time, since you won't be able to lift more than a few inches of the dough. Use your fingertips, pressing on the doubled-up dough, to seal the long edge closed.
5. Use a *rondella* (pasta cutter) to cut along the top edge of the lineup of ravioli. For these ravioli, we like to use a straight-edged cutter because that's how we've always done it, but it would also be fine to use a scal-loped-edged cutter.
6. Next, cut the individual ravioli. After each one is cut, examine the edges to make sure they are sealed. Pinch them shut anywhere you see they are slightly open and then set them in a single layer on the pre-pared sheet pans.
7. When all the ravioli are cut, pour the chicken broth into a large soup pot and add a few cups of water to fill the pot. Bring to a boil. Carefully place the ravioli in the liquid and boil until they are tender, about 10 minutes.
8. While the ravioli are boiling, melt the butter in a saucepan over low heat. Don't let the butter brown.

9. Have a large serving platter nearby. Use a handheld strainer to lift the ravioli out of the water and onto the platter. Don't worry that you are carrying some water with the ravioli. This will create a nice broth in the end. Once you have set a layer of ravioli on the platter, pour half of the melted butter over them. Sprinkle the ravioli with some Parmesan cheese. Set another layer of ravioli on top, pour more butter over them, and top with another sprinkling of cheese. You only want to put 2 layers of ravioli on each platter, so continue layering the ravioli with the butter and cheese on another platter if necessary. Serve immediately, with more grated Parmesan on the table.

"Making a dish and having it not turn out is like having a son and having him not grow up like you wanted."

—W.

Mamma is an expert at making ravioli.

FOR THE FILLING

1/2 cup cubed white bread (without crust)

Milk to cover the bread cubes

3/4 pound cleaned cod (or any sweet fish, such as shrimp, salmon, or sea bass), boiled and drained

1 tablespoon minced fresh marjoram

1 teaspoon freshly grated nutmeg

1/3 cup (about 1 ounce) freshly grated Parmesan cheese

2 large egg yolks

1/2 cup heavy cream

Salt and freshly ground black pepper

1 recipe for Fresh Pasta Dough (page 8)

FOR THE SWEET PEPPER SAUCE

12 tablespoons (1 1/2 sticks) unsalted butter

2 tablespoons extra virgin olive oil

3 scallions, minced (white parts only)

6 red bell peppers, peeled with a vegetable peeler, cored, seeds and pith removed, and diced

6 Roma tomatoes, peeled (or canned peeled whole tomatoes, drained)

1 tablespoon sugar (or more to taste)

Salt and freshly ground black pepper

3 tablespoons milk

2 tablespoons finely chopped fresh Italian parsley

Freshly grated Parmesan cheese

Fish Ravioli with Sweet Pepper Sauce
Ravioli di Merluzzo o Cernia con Salsa di Peperoni

Serves 8

In our Mediterranean diet, fish and sweet peppers are foods we eat together often. This is a nice marriage of the salty ravioli filling and the sweet pepper sauce on top.

1. Place the bread cubes in a small bowl. Cover with milk and soak for 5 minutes, until the bread is completely drenched.

2. Place the fish in the bowl of a food processor or a blender fitted with a metal blade and mix until it is almost a paste, about 15 seconds. Wring the bread cubes of excess milk and add them along with the marjoram, nutmeg, Parmesan cheese, egg yolks, and cream to the food processor with the fish. Puree until all the ingredients are combined into a paste. Transfer to a bowl and season with salt and pepper to taste. Use this filling to prepare the ravioli as instructed in steps 3, 4, 5, and 6 of Papa's Ricotta Ravioli, page 100.

3. To prepare the pepper sauce, heat 8 tablespoons of the butter and the oil in a large frying pan over medium heat. Add the scallions and sauté for about 2 minutes, until they soften. Add the red peppers and sauté 2 minutes. Add the tomatoes, sugar, and salt and pepper to taste and cook for 20 minutes, until the peppers are very tender. As you cook the peppers, taste for sugar and add more if desired, and add a splash of water if the pan is dry.

4. Transfer the cooked vegetables to the bowl of a food processor or blender fitted with a metal blade. Add the milk and puree until creamy. Pour the pepper cream back into the frying pan over low heat. Cut the remaining 4 tablespoons of butter into small pieces, add them to the pan with the pepper cream, and cook on low heat, stirring constantly, until the butter is melted. Turn off the heat.

5. Meanwhile, bring a large saucepan of water to a boil. Stir in a small fistful of salt. Carefully drop the ravioli into the water and boil until they are al dente. Carefully lift them out of the water with a handheld strainer, transfer them to the frying pan with the sauce, and place over low heat. Simmer the ravioli in the sauce for 1 minute. Transfer to a serving platter, sprinkle with the parsley, and serve immediately. Pass the Parmesan.

Ravioli with Ricotta, Potatoes, and Pancetta
Ravioli di Ricotta, Patate e Pancetta

Serves 8

Ravioli are always for special occasions. It feels festive to make them and to eat them. My brother, Paolo, loves potatoes, so Mamma invented this for him as an alternative to the standard ricotta filling. —G.

1. Boil the potatoes in salted water until they are tender when pierced with a fork. Pass them through a food mill, still warm, into a large bowl.

2. Melt half of the butter with 1 tablespoon of water in a large frying pan over medium heat. Add the onion and cook until soft and translucent, about 10 minutes. Add the pancetta and cook for 3 minutes until it is light golden. Add to the bowl with the pureed potatoes. Add the ricotta and the eggs and stir to mix well. Stir in a third of the grated Parmesan cheese, the nutmeg, and salt and pepper to taste.

3. Use this filling to prepare the ravioli as described in steps 3, 4, 5, and 6 of Papa's Ricotta Ravioli, page 100.

4. Bring a large saucepan of water to a boil. Stir in a small fistful of salt. Carefully add the ravioli and boil until al dente.

5. While the ravioli are cooking, melt but do not brown the remaining butter.

6. Remove the ravioli from the water using a handheld strainer and transfer to a large serving platter in 1 layer. Drizzle with the melted butter and sprinkle with cheese. Repeat with another layer of the ravioli; use 2 platters if necessary, as you only want to have 2 layers. Serve with more grated Parmesan.

1 3/4 pounds potatoes, peeled
1/2 pound (2 sticks) unsalted butter
1 small onion, minced
1/4 pound pancetta (or bacon), minced
1/2 pound fresh ricotta,* drained in a fine-mesh colander
2 large eggs
1 cup (about 3 ounces) freshly grated Parmesan cheese, plus more for passing at the table
1 teaspoon freshly grated nutmeg
Salt and freshly ground black pepper
1 recipe for Fresh Pasta Dough (page 8)

See source list.

Orecchiette with Lobster and Prosecco
Orecchiette con Aragosta

Serves 6

5 tablespoons unsalted butter
1/4 cup extra virgin olive oil
1 carrot, diced
1 medium red onion, halved
  and thinly sliced
1 cup prosecco (or dry spumante
  or any sparkling wine)
One 2–pound lobster, boiled and
  cut into 1-inch pieces
One 16–ounce can peeled whole
  tomatoes, drained, seeded, and
  chopped
2 cups fish stock
Salt and freshly ground black pepper
1/2 teaspoon hot pepper flakes
1 teaspoon sugar (or more to taste)
3 tablespoons finely chopped fresh
  Italian parsley
1 pound orecchiette

ORECCHIETTE,
which means "little ears," is the glory
of Puglia, the region that comprises
Italy's boot heel. This pasta is most
famous for its role in the dish *orecchiette con cime di rapa*, which translates
as "little ears and turnip tops,"
though the *cime di rapa* is not turnip
tops at all, but broccoli rabe.

The Mediterranean Sea is known for producing very tasty seafood—maybe because it is a closed sea, so the waters are concentrated. Our Sicilian lobsters come from off an island called Favagnana, to the west, and the Aeolian Islands, to the north. They are small compared to American lobsters, but they are very tasty. You can use champagne or any sparkling wine for this. We use prosecco, to be patriotic.

1. Melt the butter with the oil in a large saucepan over medium heat. Add the carrot and onion and sauté for about 3 minutes, until the onion softens and browns slightly. Add the prosecco and cook until the alcohol evaporates. Add the lobster and tomatoes and cook for a few minutes. Pour in the fish stock, a little at a time, letting it evaporate before adding more. Add the salt, pepper, hot pepper, and sugar and cook a few more minutes. Taste for seasoning and add more salt, pepper, or sugar if desired. Cook for about 10 more minutes. Stir in the parsley, reserving a little to sprinkle over the finished dish.

2. In the meantime, bring a large saucepan of water to a boil. Stir in a small fistful of salt and the orecchiette. Boil the pasta, stirring from time to time so the pasta doesn't stick together, until it is tender. Save a cupful of the pasta water and drain the pasta quickly in a colander.

3. Transfer the pasta and a splash of the pasta water to the pot with the lobster *condimento* and mix together over high heat for 2 minutes. Add more pasta water if the pasta is dry or sticky. Transfer the pasta to a pasta bowl, sprinkle with the remaining parsley, and serve right away.

Glutton's Tortiglioni
I Tortiglioni del Goloso

Serves 6

This dish has so much meat in it, it's something we only serve for special occasions, or on a Sunday afternoon when we are having friends for lunch. Since you need to open a bottle of prosecco to make it, it seems necessary that you serve it with a glass of prosecco.

TIP Our butcher does not grind chicken, so if we want it ground or minced, we boil it for about 2 minutes, then put it in the food processor to mince it. This way we can also control how minced it is.

1. Heat the butter and oil together in a very large frying pan over medium heat until the butter is melted. Add the pancetta and fry until it is golden brown, about 5 minutes. Add the onions and sauté for about 5 minutes more, until they are tender and light golden brown. Add the ground or minced chicken and fry it for 3 minutes, then add the ground beef and fry the meats for about 5 minutes, until they are cooked through and golden brown. Add a little water to the pan if the meats are sticking. Add the sparkling wine and cook until you can smell that the alcohol has evaporated. Stir in the cream, turn the heat up to high, and boil the cream for a few minutes. Add the nutmeg, salt, and pepper to taste.

2. Meanwhile, bring a large saucepan of water to a boil. Stir in a small fistful of salt and the tortiglioni and cook the pasta until it is tender. Reserve a cupful of the pasta water and drain the pasta quickly through a colander.

3. Put the pasta and a splash of pasta water in the frying pan with the meat *condimento* and mix together over high heat for about 2 minutes to warm. Add more pasta water if the pasta is sticky. Transfer the pasta to a serving bowl and serve hot with freshly grated Parmesan cheese on the table.

6 tablespoons unsalted butter
1/2 cup extra virgin olive oil
1/4 pound pancetta (or bacon),
    cut into 1/2-inch cubes
4 spring onions (white part only),
    finely chopped, or shallots
1/2 pound ground or minced bone-
    less, skinless chicken breast
1/2 pound ground beef
1 cup prosecco or spumante
    (sparkling Italian wine)
2 cups heavy cream
A few gratings nutmeg (or a pinch of
    ground nutmeg)
Salt and freshly ground black pepper
1 pound tortiglioni
Freshly grated Parmesan cheese

TORTIGLIONI
is a short, ridged, tube-shaped pasta. We often use it in baked dishes or fried as leftovers. It is not a pasta that we would eat without a *condimento*, the way we might have spaghetti with butter and Parmesan. Tortiglioni, like rigatoni, is so thick, it needs a sauce. You can use rigatoni, penne, or lumache in its place.

"Cream is a sort of medicine for cook-ing. It can make even an untasty sauce taste good."

—W.

Maccheroncini with Marsala, Chicken, and Prosciutto Cotto "For Hunters"
I Maccheroncini del Cacciatore

Serves 6

8 tablespoons (1 stick) unsalted butter
1/2 cup extra virgin olive oil, plus
  more for the pasta water
2 carrots, finely chopped
2 celery stalks, finely chopped
1 medium white or yellow onion,
  finely chopped
1/2 pound ground beef
1/4 pound prosciutto cotto (cooked
  ham), cut into 1/4-inch pieces
Salt and freshly ground black pepper
1 cup dry Marsala wine
1 small whole chicken, cut into 8
  pieces, skin removed
1 pound maccheroncini strands,
  broken into two pieces
1/4 cup finely chopped fresh Italian
  parsley
Freshly grated Parmesan cheese

TIP When you cook ground beef, it tends to form little balls that harden as you cook them. So use a fork to mash the little balls while you're cooking the meat; this helps keep the meat soft and tender.

The word **MACCHERONCINI** means "little maccheroni." It is a very long, thin pasta, like spaghetti, but with a hole in it. It is similar to the most primitive dried pasta, invented by nomadic Arabian people.
 If you can't find it, use only thick, long pasta in its place, like linguine.

Marsala is a wine from western Sicily. It is a very good wine, but nobody thought to export it until the late nineteenth century, when Englishmen living in western Sicily and working in the wine export business discovered it. Cooking with Marsala gives any dish a very special, distinct flavor, a little bit like sherry; you have to taste it to know. You can buy dry Marsala, sweet Marsala, or Marsala that is just for cooking. My mamma named this dish "For Hunters" because in Italy hunters tend to be society people, a little bit fancy, like this dish. When I was a child, we used to have big hunting parties, especially for the first day of the season. Papa and the other men would leave at dawn and Mamma and Granny would start at the same time in the kitchen to prepare a big feast for when the men returned. The hunters liked to have a complicated pasta with a lot of sauce, like this dish. —G.

TIP For this pasta, make sure to have the butcher cut the whole chicken into separate pieces and remove and discard the breast bone.

1. Warm the butter and oil in a large saucepan over medium heat. Add the carrots, celery, and onions and cook until they are soft, about 10 minutes. Add the ground beef and cook, stirring from time to time and breaking the meat up until it is cooked through. Add the ham and sauté for 5 minutes, until golden. Add salt and pepper to taste.
2. Add the Marsala to the frying pan and let it cook for a few minutes to evaporate the alcohol. Add the chicken and 2 tablespoons of water. Cover and cook on low heat until the chicken is cooked through, about 30 minutes, adding water from time to time to keep the chicken or vegetables from sticking to the pan. Remove the pan from the heat.
3. Take the chicken out of the pan. When it's cool enough to touch, pull the meat off the bone into bite-size pieces and discard the bones. Return the chicken meat to the pan and stir to combine with the *soffritto* (cooked vegetables).

4. Meanwhile, bring a large saucepan of water to a boil. Stir in a small fistful of salt, a splash of olive oil, and the maccheroncini. Stir the pasta immediately after adding it to the water and cook until tender, stirring occasionally to prevent it from sticking together. Reserve a cupful of the pasta water and drain the pasta in a colander.

5. Put the pasta and about 1/4 cup of hot pasta water into the pan with the *condimento* over high heat and stir to coat the pasta. Add the parsley and add more pasta water until the pasta is very slippery. Transfer to a serving dish and serve immediately with Parmesan cheese on the table.

The butcher's counter

Ziti with Lamb, Lemon, and Rosemary
Ziti al Profumi d'Agnello

Serves 6

This dish must be started a day in advance so the lamb has time to marinate. Because of the shape of the ziti, the sauce will get all over the tablecloth, so we suggest you serve this at an open-air lunch—with close friends! You may be surprised to see lamb and pork in the same dish, but it is not an uncommon combination in Italy, and the two meats taste wonderful together.

1 cup extra virgin olive oil
Salt and freshly ground black pepper
10 to 12 fresh bay leaves
3 lemons, sliced into thin rounds
1 medium white or yellow onion
8 sprigs rosemary
1 pound lamb, cut into 1/4-inch-thick slices
1 boneless pork chop
1 pound ziti, broken in three pieces if long
Freshly grated Parmesan cheese for sprinkling on the pasta and for passing at the table

"We have bay laurel trees growing all around Gangivecchio, one right at the foot of the steps outside the kitchen in the courtyard of the abbey. We use fresh bay laurel often in cooking, and the dried leaves make a fragrant kindling for the fireplaces, something most appreciated by our friend and agent, Janis, who lights the fireplaces in her cottage even in the summer months."

—G.

1. Pour 2 tablespoons of the oil into a baking dish big enough to marinate the meat. Add salt and pepper, a third of the bay leaves, half the lemon slices, half the onion slices, half the rosemary, and half of the lamb slices. Repeat, laying the pork on top of the lamb. Finish with a drizzle of oil and the remaining bay leaves. Cover the dish and place the meats in the refrigerator to marinate overnight.

2. Preheat oven to 300°F. Pull the lamb and pork out of the marinade, reserving the marinade. Place the meats in a layer on a baking pan and roast until they are tender and cooked to medium. Remove the meat from the oven. When it is cool enough to touch, chop it into coarse chunks. Put the chunks, along with the cooking liquid and marinade, into the bowl of a food processor fitted with a metal blade. Pulse many times, until the meats are ground like ground beef. Adjust salt and pepper to taste.

3. While the meat is roasting, bring a large saucepan of water to a boil. Stir in a small fistful of salt and the ziti and boil, stirring occasionally, until the pasta is tender. Reserve 2 cups of the pasta water and drain the ziti quickly through a colander. Put the pasta back in the pot you cooked it in. Add the chopped meat and 1/2 cup of the pasta water and stir the pasta with the *condimento* over medium heat for 2 minutes, adding more pasta water if necessary. Transfer the pasta to a serving bowl, sprinkle with Parmesan cheese, and serve immediately. Pass the Parmesan.

Mixed Seafood with Egg Fettuccine
Fettuccine all'Uovo con Pesce

Serves 6

With so many types of shellfish in this dish, it is a tribute to the fruits of our sea.

1. Wash the mussels very well in fresh water. Put them in a large saucepan with the wine, 1 garlic clove, and the parsley. Cover and cook over high heat, shaking the pan from time to time, until the mussels open. Remove the mussels with a slotted spoon, reserving the liquid. Remove the meat from the mussel shells. Discard the shells and place the mussels in a bowl. Strain the cooking liquid into the bowl and set aside.

2. Rinse the anchovy fillets with water to remove the salt. Heat the olive oil with the remaining garlic clove in a large frying pan over medium heat. Add the anchovy fillets and cook, stirring with a wooden spoon, until the anchovies disintegrate. Add the salmon and calamari and sauté for 5 minutes, or until the calamari are tender and the salmon is cooked through. Pour in the vermouth and cook for about 2 minutes, just to burn off the alcohol. Add the tomato paste plus 2 tablespoons of hot water and stir to dissolve the paste. Add the shrimp and salt to taste, and cook for about 10 minutes, until the shrimp are cooked through. Add the butter and the mussels and their liquid. Adjust the salt and pepper to taste and keep on the lowest possible heat while the pasta cooks.

3. Meanwhile, bring a large saucepan of water to a boil. Stir in a small fistful of salt, a splash of olive oil, and the fettuccine and cook until the pasta is al dente. Lift the fettuccine out of the water and into the pan with the seafood. Sprinkle with the chives, increase the heat to high, and toss the pasta with the *condimento* for about 2 minutes, to warm through, adding hot pasta water if the pasta is dry or sticky. Transfer to a serving bowl and serve immediately.

2 pounds mussels
1/2 cup dry white wine
2 garlic cloves
1/3 cup finely chopped fresh
  Italian parsley
3 anchovy fillets packed in salt
3/4 cup extra virgin olive oil,
  plus more for the pasta water
One 6-ounce salmon fillet,
  skinned and cut into cubes
3/4 pound calamari, thinly sliced
1/2 cup dry vermouth
3 tablespoons tomato paste
1/2 pound small shrimp, peeled
  and deveined
Salt and freshly ground black pepper
4 tablespoons (1/2 stick) unsalted
  butter
1 1/4 pounds egg fettuccine
2 tablespoons minced chives

"Cooking well is not easy. It's like making music. It's not about how much of this, how much of that. You either feel it or you don't."

—*W.*

PASTA FOR CATS AND DOGS

Since I was a little girl, animals have been an important presence in my life. I cannot think of any moments of my journey in this world with– out a dog or a cat beside me. My first dog, Mister, was a white and brown volpino who showed me the happiness that comes from just being together, and the gratitude for a dish of food at the end of the day. To nourish animals is as important to me as nourishing a human being. I believe that when I cook, I transmit all the love I have for my family and relatives through my hands and into the food. For this reason, every day, morning and night, before I prepare my own meal, I cook a dish of pasta for my little, faithful friends. My red–haired cat, Billy, sits motionless and watches my every movement from the top of the refrigerator while I prepare a soup of chicken, spaghetti, and broth. My tiny dog Mike, that I rescued from the street, is crazy for spaghetti and tomato sauce. My wise dog, Silla, patiently waits for his pasta and meat. My dog Blue, whom we saved from a cruel destiny, is so grateful to sit in front of his short pasta and chicken. Through them I continue to feed all the animals I had and lost, all the animals I will have in the time allowed me.

To make pasta for your cats and dogs, fill a small pan with cold water. Add chicken breasts in measure of 2 ounces for every small dog or cat. Boil. When the chicken is cooked, take it out of the pan. In the same water, put the spaghetti or capellini—again, 2 ounces for each small dog or cat—and boil. While the pasta is boiling, cut the chicken into very small pieces. Cook the pasta until it is very tender. Drain and cut it into small pieces. Combine the pasta with the chicken pieces, divide it among the individual dishes, sprinkle with a teaspoon of grated Parmesan cheese, and serve to your humble, hungry, and loyal friends.   —W.

Knowing how much we love animals, Carolina brought her curious cat, George, to stay with us at Gangivecchio.

Mezze Penne Rigate with Pork Ragù and Swiss Chard
Mezze Penne Rigate con Ragù di Maiale e Giri

Serves 6

We love Swiss chard, and we have tons—it grows wild here at Gangivecchio and is widely available in the markets. It's very traditional to pair these greens with meat as we do in this recipe. If you have green beans, you can cut them in little pieces and use them in place of the chard.

1. To clean the Swiss chard, soak it in a sink or bowl full of water, changing the water several times until there is no dirt at the bottom. Pull the leaves off the stems and discard the stems. Coarsely chop the chard with the wild fennel.

2. Heat 1 cup of the olive oil in a big saucepan over medium heat. Add the onion and sauté for about 3 minutes, or until it begins to soften. Add the chopped chard and fennel and the bay leaf, stir, and cook for 5 minutes or until the chard is tender, adding hot water to the pan if it is dry. Add the ground pork and cook until it loses its pink color. Add the wine and salt and pepper to taste and cook for about 3 minutes to cook off the alcohol taste. Add the tomato sauce and the basil and simmer over low heat for 1 hour, adding hot water to the pan if necessary.

3. Meanwhile, bring a big saucepan of water to a boil. Add a small fistful of salt and the pasta and boil until tender. Save a cupful of the pasta water, drain in a colander, and quickly add the pasta to the pan with the *condimento*.

4. While the pasta is cooking, put the breadcrumbs in a frying pan with the remaining 1/4 cup of olive oil and toast for 2 to 3 minutes over medium heat until the breadcrumbs are softer. Add the garlic and sauté for 1 minute, stirring constantly. Turn off the heat and stir in the grated pecorino and the parsley and cook for another minute. Sprinkle the mixture over the pasta and toss together over high heat for 1 or 2 minutes to warm through. Serve immediately, with more grated pecorino on the table.

2 pounds Swiss chard
3/4 pound fennel bulb and fronds or wild fennel fronds
1 1/4 cup extra virgin olive oil
1 medium white or yellow onion, chopped
1 fresh bay leaf
1 pound ground pork
1 cup red wine
Salt and freshly ground black pepper
2 1/2 cups Fresh Tomato Sauce (page 9; or bottled sauce*)
1/2 cup finely chopped fresh basil
1 pound mezze penne rigate
1/4 cup breadcrumbs
2 garlic cloves, minced
3 tablespoons (about 1 ounce) freshly grated pecorino cheese, plus more for passing at the table
1/2 cup finely chopped fresh Italian parsley

*See source list.

MEZZE PENNE RIGATE
means "half penne rigate," because they are half the length of regular penne. If you can't find it, penne rigate, or any short pasta, will work fine.

Spaghetti with Sea Urchin
Spaghetti con Ricci di Mondello

Serves 4

From early spring to early fall, it is very popular for Palermitani, those who live in Palermo, to visit the seaside community of Mondello. There you will find outdoor restaurants all along the waterside, every one of which claims to serve the very best spaghetti con ricci. I got this recipe from my friend Paolo, because I knew there was no way that a restaurant would give me their true recipe. To have the full taste of sea urchin eggs, you must not cook them.

TIP For this pasta, the sea urchin roe is not cooked. It relies on the heat of the spaghetti to warm it, which means you must have the table set and everyone *a tavola* before you begin to cook the spaghetti.

TIP The best way to get the eggs out of the sea urchins is to ask your fishmonger to do it for you.

1/2 cup extra virgin olive oil, plus more to add to the pasta water
2 garlic cloves
1/2 cup finely chopped fresh Italian parsley, plus more to sprinkle on the pasta
1 1/3 cups sea urchin roe
Salt and freshly ground black pepper
1 pound spaghetti

1. Pour the oil into a heatproof cup and place it in a pot of hot but not boiling water, to heat it without cooking away any of the olive taste.

2. Crush the garlic very well using a mortar and pestle, or mince it very fine. Scrape it into the bottom of the bowl you will serve the pasta in. Add the parsley, the warm olive oil, and salt and black pepper to taste and stir it all together. Add the sea urchin roe and let this rest while you cook the spaghetti.

3. Bring a big saucepan of water to a boil. Stir in a small fistful of salt and a splash of olive oil. Add the spaghetti and stir. Boil the spaghetti, stirring often to prevent it from sticking together, until it is al dente. Lift the spaghetti out of the water using a spaghetti strainer and place it directly into the bowl with the roe. Don't worry if a little water comes with the spaghetti into the serving bowl; the hot pasta water will help the texture of the *condimento*. Toss the spaghetti with the roe, adding more pasta water if necessary. Sprinkle with more parsley and serve immediately.

Mondello-Style Spaghetti with Lobster
Spaghetti con L'Aragosta

Serves 4

The terrible thing about cooking lobster is that, unlike any other food, you have to kill the lobster yourself first. We have a saying in Italian: "Occhio che non vede, cuore che non duole." "Eye that doesn't see, heart that doesn't burn." With this, we prefer to eat lobster in restaurants rather than at home. But if you are dying to prepare spaghetti with lobster at home, the first thing to do is buy 2 live lobsters and carry them home. Once you are all in the kitchen, forget that the lobsters are still moving, rinse them under cold water, and then put them on a cutting surface. Holding the lobster with one hand and a big sharp knife in the other, chop the pincers from each side of the body. Then cut across the length of the tail in 5 or 6 pieces and cut the body in 2 parts lengthwise. Remove and throw away the little bag that contains sand. Now here you are, ready to make dinner.

1. In a large frying pan, heat 1/2 cup of the oil over medium heat. Add the onion and sauté until transparent and tender, about 3 minutes. Add the tomatoes, sugar, and salt and pepper to taste and cook for about 15 minutes, until the tomatoes break down. You may need to add just a little water if the tomatoes begin to stick to the pan. Taste the sauce and add more salt, pepper, or sugar if you desire.

2. In another large frying pan, heat the remaining 1/2 cup of olive oil with the garlic cloves. Add the lobster pieces and sauté for 5 minutes, until the shells of the lobster become bright red. Add the wine and cook until it evaporates. Transfer the lobster and all the pan juices to the pan with the tomato sauce. Sprinkle with the parsley and cook the sauce with the lobster for 15 minutes more. If you are using cream, stir it in at this point and cook it with the tomato sauce for about 1 minute.

3. Meanwhile, bring a large saucepan of water to a boil. Add a small fistful of salt and a splash of olive oil. Stir in the spaghetti and boil until the spaghetti is al dente, stirring from time to time to keep the spaghetti from sticking together.

4. Take the lobster out of the tomato sauce and place it on a plate or bowl. Lift the spaghetti out of the pasta water with a spaghetti strainer and transfer it directly into the frying pan with the tomato sauce over high heat. Toss the pasta with the sauce for 1 or 2 minutes to warm, adding enough pasta water so the *condimento* is wet and slippery. Trans-

"In Italy, we say that if there's something wrong with a dish, you add cream and it is fixed. You can add cream to this and it may be even tastier, but I think you lose a little taste of the sea."

—G.

1 cup extra virgin olive oil, plus more for the pasta water

1/2 medium white or yellow onion, chopped

One 28-ounce can peeled whole tomatoes, drained in a colander and broken up with your hands

2 teaspoons sugar (or more to taste)

Salt and freshly ground black pepper

2 garlic cloves

2 small lobsters, prepared as described above

1/2 cup dry white wine

1/2 cup finely chopped fresh Italian parsley

2–3 tablespoons heavy cream (optional)

1 pound spaghetti

fer the spaghetti to a flat serving platter or onto individual dishes and top with the lobster pieces. Serve immediately.

TIP Though it's a little less grand to look at, to make this pasta easier to eat, while the pasta is cooking, remove the lobster meat from the shells. Then add the chunks of lobster to the tomato sauce before toss–ing the sauce with the pasta.

Dried fava beans, perfect for soup

Tagliatelle with Dried Fava Beans and Leafy Green Vegetables
Tagliatelle con Fave Secche e Verdure

Serves 6

The fava beans and these types of greens really ask for oil, so we like to drizzle olive oil on this pasta after it is tossed with the condimento. *The truth is that there is no pasta that wouldn't taste good with olive oil drizzled over it. When we do this, we always use the best, fruitiest olive oil we have.*

1. To clean the greens, soak them in a sink or an enormous bowl full of water, changing the water many times until no dirt falls to the bottom. While the greens are soaking, remove their tough stems with your hands. Drain, stack the leaves together, and cut them into strips about 1 inch wide.

2. Heat the oil in a large soup pot over medium heat. Add the onion and sauté until soft and translucent, about 5 minutes. Add the greens, mix them with the oil and onions, and sauté for 3 minutes, until they wilt and reduce in size significantly. Add the drained fava beans and salt and pepper; cover with hot water, and simmer the favas with the greens for 1 1/2 to 2 hours, until the favas are tender. You may need to add water from time to time. When the favas are tender and the liquid has evaporated, turn off the heat.

3. Bring a large saucepan of water to a boil. Stir in a small fistful of salt and a splash of olive oil. Break the tagliatelle in half into the water and cook until the pasta is tender, stirring from time to time to prevent sticking. Reserve a cupful of the pasta water and drain the tagliatelle in a colander.

4. Quickly transfer the tagliatelle to the pan with the favas and greens; don't worry if there is still some water on the pasta, the *condimento* will want it. Stir the pasta with the *condimento* over high heat, adding more hot pasta water if the *condimento* does not easily coat the pasta. Transfer to a large serving bowl, drizzle with olive oil, sprinkle with the grated pecorino cheese, and serve immediately, with more pecorino on the table.

2 pounds mixed dark leafy greens, such as Swiss chard, borage, chicory, kale, mustard, or collard greens

1 cup olive oil, plus more for the pasta water and for drizzling over the finished dish

1 medium white or yellow onion, chopped

3/4 pound dried fava beans, soaked overnight and drained

Salt and freshly ground black pepper

1 pound fresh tagliatelle

1/4 cup freshly grated pecorino cheese, plus more for the table

Ditaloni with Eggplant Balls, Potato, and Pancetta
Ditaloni con Polpettine di Melanzane, Patate e Pancetta

Serves 8

We serve this dish in the restaurant with the pasta on a large platter surrounded by the polpettine. It's a nice way to present the pasta, and it is very much appreciated by our guests. Although the children like this dish, they seem to like even more to hide the polpettine and, after lunch, go in the courtyard for a polpettine battle.

1/2 pound pancetta (or bacon),
   cut into 1/2-inch cubes
2 tablespoons extra virgin olive oil
1 pound potatoes, peeled and cut
   into 1/4-inch cubes
Salt and freshly ground black pepper
1/2 loaf (1/2 pound) day-old bread
2 cups whole milk
2 pounds eggplant (about 2 large),
   peeled and cut into 1/2-inch cubes
2 large egg yolks
1 cup fresh breadcrumbs
1/4 cup dried currants, soaked in
   hot water for at least 20 minutes
1/4 cup pine nuts
1/4 pound (about 1 1/3 cups) grated
   caciocavallo cheese (or provolone),
   plus more for passing at the table
Soybean oil (or other mild-flavored
   oil), for deep-frying
1 pound ditaloni

1. Cook the pancetta in a frying pan with the olive oil over high heat until the oil is hot. Add the potatoes, season with salt and pepper to taste, and sauté, stirring from time to time to prevent the potatoes from sticking, until they are golden brown and tender, 15 to 20 minutes. Taste for salt and pepper and season with more if you like.

2. Place the bread in a bowl and pour the milk over it. Wring the bread between your hands like you are handwashing clothes, so the bread falls apart and absorbs all the milk. If some pieces of the crust remain tough, throw them away.

3. While the potatoes are cooking, bring a large pot of water to a boil. Salt the water and add the eggplant cubes. Boil the eggplant until it is mushy, about 15 minutes. Drain in a colander placed in the sink and allow the eggplant to cool slightly. Press on the eggplant with your hands, a wooden spoon, or a plate to squeeze out the excess water.

4. Transfer the drained eggplant to a big mixing bowl. Add the drenched bread little by little, mixing it in with the eggplant until the mixture is the right consistency to roll into a ball with your hands. It's a matter of feel and experience. Remember that you will still add breadcrumbs, which will make the mixture drier and less sticky. Stir in the egg yolks, breadcrumbs, currants, pine nuts, half of the caciocavallo cheese, and salt and pepper to taste. Roll the dough between your palms into walnut-sized balls and place them on a platter.

5. Pour enough soybean oil into a large frying pan so it is 1 inch deep and heat over medium-high heat until it is hot enough to sizzle when you drop water into it. Prepare a platter or counter space with paper towels to drain the fried eggplant balls. Add the eggplant balls to the oil, being careful so the oil doesn't splatter, and fry, turning them in the oil, until they are golden brown all over, about 7 minutes. Lift them out of the oil with a slotted spoon and place on the paper towels to drain.

6. Meanwhile, bring a large saucepan of water to a boil. Stir in a small fistful of salt and the ditaloni and cook until the pasta is tender. Reserve a cupful of the pasta water and drain the pasta quickly through a colander. Put the pasta back in the pot you cooked it in. Add the potato and pancetta, along with any oil in the pan, and 1/4 cup of hot pasta water. Stir the pasta with the *condimento* over high heat, adding pasta water until the pasta is slippery, and cook for about 2 minutes to warm through.

7. Transfer the pasta to a serving platter and sprinkle with the remaining cheese. Arrange the eggplant balls around the edges of the platter and serve hot, with more grated cheese on the table.

"Italians are famous for going abroad and, on the third day, we miss our pasta. We are known to stash bags of pasta in our bags for when we are desperate."

—G.

A corner of the abbey

Spaghetti with Veal Bolognese
Spaghetti con Ragù di Tritato

"Ragù means any sauce with meat that cooks for a long, long time."
—G.

1 cup extra virgin olive oil, plus
  more for the pasta water
1 medium white or yellow onion,
  finely chopped
2 1/2 pounds ground veal
1 cup tomato paste
One 6-ounce piece Parmesan
  cheese rind
2 carrots, cut into four pieces
1 heaping tablespoon sugar
  (or more to taste)
2 cups vegetable broth
Salt and freshly ground black pepper
2 pounds spaghetti
A walnut of butter (about 2
  tablespoons)
Freshly grated Parmesan cheese

"Parmesan rind is something of value to us. When we grate the Parmesan, we always save the rinds to put in minestrone or ragù."
—W.

Bolognese is from Bologna originally, but now it is a favorite all over Italy. All you need to say is "Bolognese" and you know what you're getting: pasta with a rich sauce made with ground veal (or beef, or a combination). At Gangivecchio, Bolognese is always served with spaghetti, but it is also good with ditaloni. This recipe is very large because Bolognese is something we serve on Sundays, for friends. But boil only enough pasta for what you need at that time and save the rest of the Bolognese for another occasion. You can prepare the condimento 3 or 4 days ahead of time and keep it in the refrigerator.

1. Heat the olive oil over medium–high heat. Add the onions and sauté for 3 to 4 minutes, until they are tender and beginning to color. Add the veal and sauté, stirring often and breaking up the meat as it cooks, until it loses its pink color. Stir in the tomato paste, Parmesan rind, carrots, sugar, and vegetable broth and bring to a boil. Reduce the heat to low and simmer for about 1 1/2 hours, adding more water if the pan becomes dry and stirring about every 15 minutes until you have a rich, thick *ragù*. Discard the carrots and any remainig cheese rind, and taste for salt and pepper.

2. Bring a large soup pot of water to a boil. Add a small fistful of salt to taste. Stir in a splash of olive oil and the spaghetti and cook, stirring occasionally, until the spaghetti is al dente.

3. Meanwhile, pour a big ladleful of the sauce into a large serving bowl. Add the butter and a ladle of pasta water. Lift the spaghetti out of the water with a spaghetti strainer and into the bowl with the Bolognese and toss. Reserve about a cup of the sauce to top the pasta, and add the rest of the sauce and a splash of hot pasta water. Toss again, adding more pasta water until the pasta is wet and slippery. Pour the last ladle of sauce on top of the spaghetti and sprinkle with grated Parmesan cheese. Serve immediately, with more Parmesan on the table.

Rigatoni with Meat, Eggplant, and Peas in Tomato Sauce
La Pasta dei Monaci

Serves 6

One Saturday afternoon while we were working on this book, the monks who live in Gangi and other nearby towns made their annual visit. Every year they come, about 60 of them, and enjoy a big feast and a nice social time in the courtyard of the abbey. My mother made this dish for them this year. They loved it, and so we named it pasta dei monaci *after them. For us, a dish like this is a great way to use leftover meat, but if you don't have leftovers, fresh ground beef, pork, or veal cooked through in a frying pan works just fine.*

1. Pour enough olive oil into a large, deep frying pan to fill it 3 inches deep. Heat the oil until it is very hot but not smoking. (It will sizzle when you drop water in it.) Add the eggplant in batches, being careful not to overcrowd the pan, and fry until it is golden brown on all sides, about 5 minutes. Remove the eggplant with a slotted spoon and place it on a thick bed of paper towels to drain.

2. Heat the 3/4 cup oil and the onion in a large saucepan and sauté over medium heat until golden and tender, about 10 minutes. Add the meat, fried eggplant, peas, tomato sauce, and salt and pepper to taste and cook on medium-low heat for 10 to 12 minutes, stirring often, to meld the flavors together.

3. Bring a big saucepan of water to a boil over high heat. Stir in a small fistful of salt and the rigatoni and boil the pasta until it is tender. Reserve a cupful of the pasta water and drain the pasta in a colander.

4. Quickly return the pasta to the pot it was cooked in and place over high heat. Add the *condimento* and a splash of hot pasta water and mix it with the pasta, adding more pasta water if the pasta is dry or sticky and the *condimento* is not coating it smoothly. Add the caciocavallo cheese, toss, and transfer the pasta to a serving bowl. Serve immediately with grated pecorino cheese.

3/4 cup extra virgin olive oil, plus more for frying the eggplant

1 medium eggplant, cut into 1/2-inch cubes

1 small white or yellow onion, chopped

1 cup shredded leftover beef, pork, or veal (such as short ribs or hamburger), or cooked ground beef, pork, or veal

1 cup fresh or frozen green peas, cooked to tender

3/4 cup Fresh Tomato Sauce (page 9; or bottled sauce*)

Salt and freshly ground black pepper

1 pound rigatoni

3 ounces caciocavallo cheese, cut into 1/2-inch cubes (or provolone)

Freshly grated pecorino cheese for the table

*See source list.

Soup with Pasta
(Minestra)

80. Borlotti Bean and Pasta Soup
    (Pasta e Fagiole)

81. Milk Soup with Gnocchetti, Potatoes, and Parmesan
    (Minestra di Gnocchetti e Latte)

82. September Soup with Green Beans and Caciocavallo
    (Minestra di Settembre con Fagiolini e Caciocavallo)

83. Mamma's Lettuce Soup
    (Minestra di Lattuga)

84. Potato Soup with Pasta
    (Minestra di Patate con Pasta)

85. Mamma's Summer Vegetable Soup
    (Minestrone di Verdure di Mamma)

86. Hearty Lentil Soup with Ditalini
    (Minestra di Lenticchie e Ditalini)

When we make soup, we always put pasta in it. This is who we are.

TIP Adding baking soda to the water when you cook beans helps them to become softer and creamier as they cook. Even with the soup off the heat, it will bubble up when you stir in the baking soda. If you don't take it off the heat first, it may bubble up and out of the pot.

Borlotti Bean and Pasta Soup
Pasta e Fagiole

Serves 6

My mother's pasta e fagiole *is the best I've ever tasted, because she's able to make the beans creamy. Her secrets are that she soaks the beans overnight, adds baking soda while cooking them, and, most importantly, cooks the beans long enough so that they are tender and creamy inside. We traditionally use borlotti beans, which are white with red stripes (in the United States, they are often sold as cranberry beans), but you can make this soup using many different dried beans. The regular* pasta e fagiole *doesn't have hot pepper in it. That is my addition to this soup—and to just about everything.* —G.

1/4 pound pancetta (or bacon),
   cut into 1/2-inch cubes
1 medium white or yellow onion,
   chopped
1/2 cup extra virgin olive oil
3 celery stalks, chopped
2 cups dried borlotti (cranberry)
   beans, covered with cool water,
   soaked overnight, and drained
1/2 teaspoon baking soda
Salt and freshly ground black pepper
A pinch of hot pepper flakes or
   cayenne pepper
1/4 cup tomato paste
1 tablespoon sugar (or more to taste)
1/2 pound ditalini
Freshly grated Parmesan cheese

1. Place the pancetta in a large pot over medium heat and fry it for about 10 minutes, until it is golden brown and slightly crispy. Add the onions and the olive oil and cook for 10 more minutes, until the onion is soft and light golden.

2. Add the celery, drained beans, and 3 quarts of cool water. Bring the water to a boil. Take the pot off the heat to stir in the baking soda.

3. Season the soup with salt and pepper and the hot pepper. Be careful not to add too much salt at this point; the water will reduce as you cook the beans and the soup will get saltier as it does. Return the soup to medium-low heat and simmer, uncovered, until the beans are tender, about 2 hours, stirring occasionally.

4. Stir in the tomato paste and sugar and simmer the soup for about 10 minutes. Depending on how much water is left and how thick you like your soup, you may need to add some boiling water to the soup. Note that the starch from the pasta will thicken the soup even more.

5. Bring the soup to a boil over medium-high heat. Stir in the ditalini and boil the pasta in the soup, stirring very often, until the pasta is tender, about 15 minutes. Serve hot, with grated Parmesan cheese. If you have leftovers, add some boiling water and heat the soup over low heat.

TIP You must stir the soup while you cook the pasta because the beans tend to be very difficult—they like to stick to the pan.

Milk Soup with Gnocchetti, Potatoes, and Parmesan
Minestra di Gnocchetti e Latte

Serves 6

Every year, once a year, it is a tradition for my mother to invite 10 nuns from the convent of Gangi to have lunch in our restaurant. When they accept the invitation, they always request a light meal. This soup seems to be their favorite. A few years ago, the convent's new mother superior appreciated the dish so much that she drank a whole bottle of red wine in its honor. —G.

1. Heat the olive oil and butter together in a large saucepan over medium heat until the butter is melted. Add the onion and sauté for 3 minutes. Stir in the potatoes and sauté for another 3 to 4 minutes, until they begin to soften. Add the hot milk, veal broth, and salt and pepper to taste. Bring to a boil over high heat. Reduce the heat and simmer for 20 minutes, until the potatoes are very tender when pierced with a fork.
2. Add the pasta to the milk and potatoes and cook until the pasta is tender. Taste and add more salt and pepper to your liking. Pour the soup into a serving bowl. Sprinkle with Parmesan cheese and serve hot. Pass the Parmesan.

1/3 cup extra virgin olive oil
6 tablespoons (3/4 stick) unsalted butter
1 small white or yellow onion, minced
4 medium potatoes, peeled and cut into 1/2-inch cubes
5 cups boiled milk
3 cups veal or beef broth
Salt and freshly ground black pepper
1/2 pound gnocchetti
Freshly grated Parmesan cheese

September Soup with Green Beans and Caciocavallo
Minestra di Settembre con Fagiolini e Caciocavallo

Serves 6

1/2 cup extra virgin olive oil
4 tablespoons (1/2 stick) unsalted
  butter
3 garlic cloves
1 medium white or yellow onion,
  halved lengthwise
1 pound green beans, cleaned,
  trimmed, and cut into 2-inch pieces
1 tablespoon *estratto** (or tomato
  paste)
2 quarts vegetable broth
1/2 pound ditalini
1/2 teaspoon cayenne pepper
Salt
2 ounces (about 2/3 cup) caciocavallo
  cheese, grated (or provolone)

*See source list.

I love September, but it is a sort of sweet, sad good-bye, because it is the end of summer. And the winters here are very hard, something I dread every year. This soup is a comfort food to anticipate what is coming, and to celebrate the last of the summer offerings. —G.

1. Heat the oil and butter together in a large saucepan over medium-low heat until the butter is melted. Add the garlic and onion halves and sauté for 2 minutes to flavor the oil. Remove the garlic and onion and add the green beans. Turn the heat up and sauté the beans until they are tender, about 3 minutes.

2. Stir in the *estratto* and the broth and simmer for 20 minutes. Bring the broth to a boil, stir in the ditalini, and boil the pasta, stirring occasionally, until it is tender. Stir in the hot pepper and salt to taste. Pour the soup into a serving bowl and sprinkle with the caciocavallo cheese. Serve warm, with more caciocavallo on the table.

DITALINI
means "small thimbles," for its shape. Children love ditalini with fresh tomato sauce. It is often their introduction to pasta. The bigger version, ditaloni, is "only for adults," because it is too big for the children to eat easily.

Mamma's Lettuce Soup
Minestra di Lattuga

Serves 6

My mamma and I love this soup. It is quick and easy to make and also very tasty. So if you are tired or don't feel like standing in front of a boiling pot forever, this is the perfect thing. We think of lettuce as a relaxing vegetable, and this soup is something that we eat often, because we believe it makes us sleep well. We use a nice sweet, tender lettuce for this soup, something similar to what you call "butter" lettuce. —G.

TIP Whenever possible, use your hands to tear lettuce rather than chop it. The blade of the knife blackens the lettuce and ruins the taste.

1. Remove the lettuce leaves from the core and clean them very well. Use your hands to tear the lettuce into large pieces.

2. Combine the vegetable broth and 2 quarts of water in a large saucepan and bring to a boil over high heat. Add the garlic cloves, reduce the heat, and simmer for 2 minutes. Add the lettuce, and salt to taste. When the lettuce is just tender but still a little crunchy under your teeth, add the broken spaghetti, stir, and simmer until the pasta is tender. Adjust the salt to taste. Transfer the soup to a serving bowl, sprinkle with the Parmesan cheese, and wait 5 minutes before serving, so the cheese will melt in the broth. Pass more Parmesan at the table.

2 heads butter lettuce (or other sweet, tender leaf lettuce)
1 quart vegetable broth
3 garlic cloves
Salt
1/4 pound spaghetti, broken into 2-inch-long pieces (or ditalini or ditaloni)
1/3 cup (about 1 ounce) freshly grated Parmesan cheese, plus more for the table

I love **BROKEN SPAGHETTI** because it reminds me of my childhood. There weren't very many short pasta shapes back then, so to get a small pasta that was easy for a child to eat, my mamma used to break the spaghetti into small pieces. To break any long pasta, we wrap it in a kitchen cloth, then bend the cloth so that the pasta breaks into many pieces but stays neatly inside the cloth. Then we open the cloth over the boiling water for the pasta to spill into the pot when we are ready. —W.

Potato Soup with Pasta
Minestra di Patate con Pasta

Like so many soups, this is especially good in the winter. But we also like it in the summer, served either room temperature or cold.

1/4 cup extra virgin olive oil
2 pounds potatoes, peeled and
   cut into 1/2–inch cubes
1 medium white or yellow onion,
   chopped
One 3–ounce piece of Parmesan
   cheese rind
Salt and freshly ground black pepper
1 quart vegetable broth
1/4 cup tomato paste
1 1/2 cups ditalini
2 tablespoons finely chopped
   fresh Italian parsley
Freshly grated Parmesan or
   pecorino cheese

1. Bring 2 quarts of water to a boil. Meanwhile, heat the olive oil in a large soup pot over medium heat. Add the potatoes, onion, and cheese rind and sauté for 3 to 4 minutes, until the onion has begun to soften. Season lightly with salt and pepper. Add the vegetable broth and bring it to a boil over medium heat. Reduce the heat and simmer for about 10 minutes. Stir in the tomato paste and simmer for another 15 minutes.
2. Stir in half of the boiling water and bring it back to a boil. Add the ditalini. Cook the ditalini at a low boil, stirring often so the soup doesn't stick to the pan, until the pasta is tender. Add more boiling water if the soup is too thick. Turn off the heat. Remove and discard any remains of the cheese rind. Taste for salt and pepper and add more to taste. Trans–fer the soup to a large serving bowl or individual soup bowls. Sprinkle with the parsley and grated cheese. Serve immediately with more grated cheese at the table.

Fresh cheese hangs in a shop window in Gangi.

Mamma's Summer Vegetable Soup
Minestrone di Verdure di Mamma

Serves 8

Minestrone is my mother's triumph. In the summertime, she makes it with all the vegetables we have in our home garden—it's a sort of ritual to see her in the kitchen cutting the zucchini, carrots, potatoes, and onions into cubes. It's common to make this soup with pasta, as we do all soups. But it is also elegant to serve it without, with just a bowl of freshly made croutons on the table to float in the soup. —G.

1. Heat the olive oil in a large soup pot over medium heat. Add the potatoes, carrots, celery, and onions and sauté 3 or 4 minutes, until the onion is translucent and just beginning to color. Add the spinach, tomatoes, green beans, peas, garlic, basil, and Parmesan cheese rind and sauté for about 5 minutes, until the vegetables begin to soften. Be careful not to let the garlic brown. Season lightly with salt and pepper.

2. Add the broth and 2 cups of water and bring it to a boil over high heat. Reduce the heat and simmer the soup for 30 to 40 minutes, or until the vegetables are tender, adding more water if the soup is too thick. Bring it to a boil. Add the ditalini or spaghetti if desired, and cook until the pasta is tender. Stir in the hot pepper and more salt and pepper to taste. Transfer to a serving bowl and sprinkle with the parsley. Serve hot, with Parmesan cheese and pepper-infused oil on the table.

1/2 cup extra virgin olive oil

1 1/4 pounds potatoes, peeled and cubed

2 large carrots, diced

3 celery stalks, thinly sliced

1 medium white or yellow onion, chopped

2 bunches fresh spinach, washed, stems removed, and drained

1 1/2 pounds fresh tomatoes, peeled and chopped

1 pound green beans, ends removed, cut into 1-inch pieces

1 cup frozen or fresh shelled green peas

1 garlic clove, minced

1 *ciuffo* of fresh basil leaves (15 to 20 leaves), chopped

One 3-ounce piece Parmesan cheese rind

Salt and freshly ground black pepper

2 quarts vegetable broth

1/4 pound ditalini or broken spaghetti (optional)

Pinch of cayenne pepper or hot pepper flakes

2 tablespoons finely chopped fresh Italian parsley

Freshly grated Parmesan cheese

Pepper-infused olive oil for the table

Hearty Lentil Soup with Ditalini
Minestra di Lenticchie e Ditalini

Serves 6

We have lentils in Sicily that are famous. They're from the island of Ustica, but they're very difficult to find even for us; we can only find them in gourmet stores. You can use any lentils for this, but if you can find lenticchie di Ustica, you will be very pleased. The same word—lenticchie—is used for "freckles" in the Sicilian dialect.

2 pounds lentils, soaked overnight, drained, and rinsed
1 medium potato, peeled and diced
2 medium white or yellow onions, diced
2 carrots, diced
1/2 teaspoon baking soda
1 cup extra virgin olive oil
1/4 cup tomato paste
Salt and freshly ground black pepper
Pinch of cayenne pepper or hot pepper flakes
1 cup chopped dark green fennel tops or wild fennel
1 1/2 cups ditalini
Best-quality olive oil for drizzling on the soup
Freshly grated Parmesan cheese

Put the lentils, potato, onions, and carrots into a large soup pot with enough cool water to cover by 1 inch. Bring the water to a boil over high heat. Remove the pot from the heat and stir in the baking soda. The baking soda may cause the water to foam up, but the foam will fall. When the foaming has begun to die down, return the pot to the heat and stir in the olive oil, tomato paste, a light amount of salt and pepper, and the cayenne or pepper flakes. Reduce the heat and simmer the soup until the lentils are tender, 30 minutes or more. Add enough water so that the soup is the desired thickness and bring it to a boil over high heat. Add the fennel and the ditalini and cook until the pasta is tender, about 15 minutes. Adjust the salt and pepper to taste. Let the soup rest, off the heat, for about 10 minutes before serving. Top each serving with a swirl of your best olive oil and pass the Parmesan at the table.

TIP When you're adding hot pepper to a sauce or *condimento*, add a little at a time, then taste. When you have just a hint of burning in your mouth, it's the right amount.

Baked Pastas and Timballos
(Pasta al Forno e Timballo)

87. Baked Orecchiette with Lamb Ragù and Melted Mozzarella
    (*Orecchiette con Ragù di Agnello al Forno*)

88. Fresh Cod and Zucchini Lasagne
    (*Lasagne con Zucchine e Merluzzo*)

89. Classic Baked Lasagne
    (*Lasagne Pasticciate Classiche*)

90. Paolo's Pesto Lasagne
    (*Lasagne con il Pesto del Cavaliere*)

91. Orietta's Baked Penne Casserole with Leeks and Green Peas
    (*Pasticcio di Penne al Forno di Orietta*)

92. Maccheroni Gratinée with Olives and Tomatoes
    (*Maccheroni con Pomodoro e Olive Gratinati*)

93. Cannelloni with Vegetable–Ricotta Filling
    (*Cannelloni con Verdure e Ricotta*)

94. Baked Timballo of Anelletti with Veal and Vegetables
    (*Anelletti al Forno*)

*B*aked pastas and timballos are always for a special occasion. They are a thing for holidays, for Sunday afternoons when you have a big table of friends for a late lunch, for picnics and parties. There is something wonderful about a baked pasta—when you take it out of the oven, it is like the moment of victory for all the effort you put into it. A timballo is also always something special and sensual. When you set it on the table, it seems very unique, and when you cut into it, all the flavors come steaming out.

Baked Orecchiette with Lamb Ragù and Melted Mozzarella
Orecchiette con Ragù di Agnello al Forno

Serves 4

Our lamb is so tender and tasty. It is something we have only in the spring, and we relish it during the short time it is available. Try to find young, farm-raised lamb for this.

1/2 cup extra virgin olive oil, plus more for greasing the baking dish and for the pasta water
1 small white or yellow onion, halved and sliced
10 ounces ground lamb
3/4 pound ripe tomatoes, chopped
Salt and freshly ground black pepper
3/4 pound orecchiette
1 cup (about 3 ounces) grated pecorino cheese, plus more to pass at the table
2 tablespoons unsalted butter
1/2 pound fresh mozzarella, sliced

1. Preheat the oven to 450°F. Grease a large casserole dish (approximately 8 × 10 inches) with olive oil.

2. Warm the 1/2 cup olive oil in a saucepan over medium–low heat. Add the onion slices and sauté until light golden, about 3 minutes. Add the lamb and sauté until it is golden brown, about 3 minutes more. Stir in the tomatoes and salt and pepper to taste. Reduce the heat to low and continue to cook for 20 minutes, adding a splash of water from time to time if the lamb is sticking to the pan.

3. Meanwhile, bring a large saucepan of water to a boil. Stir in a small fistful of salt and a splash of olive oil. Add the orecchiette and cook until tender, stirring often during the cooking, as orecchiette tend to stick together. Save a cupful of the pasta water, drain the pasta in a colander, and return it to the pan you cooked it in.

4. Add the lamb *ragù* to the pan with the pasta, 2 tablespoons of the grated pecorino, the butter, and 1/2 cup (or more) pasta water and mix well.

5. Spread a third of the pasta in 1 even layer in the prepared baking dish. Sprinkle with a third of the remaining pecorino and some slices of mozzarella. Repeat in 2 more layers to use all the ingredients. Place the baking dish in the oven and bake the pasta for 20 minutes or until the top is golden brown. Turn on the broiler and broil the pasta for 1 minute, to form a nice crust. Serve in the same dish, with grated pecorino on the table.

Fresh Cod and Zucchini Lasagne
Lasagne con Zucchine e Merluzzo

Serves 6

Cod is one of the favorite fish of this area. The union with the zucchini is perfect, because the cod has such a strong flavor and the zucchini is mild and sweet. It is a way to take humble ingredients and make a very elegant dish. We make this in a pirofila, which is what we call a baking dish that you can put in the oven and that is also nice enough to put on the table.

1. Preheat the oven to 350°F. Butter a heatproof casserole dish (approximately 9 × 12 inches) that is nice enough to serve at the table.

2. Pour the vegetable broth and bay leaves into a large, deep sauté pan and bring to a boil over high heat. Reduce the heat, place the cod fillets in the pan, and simmer for about 10 minutes, until the fish turns white. Turn off the heat and let the fish sit in the broth while you prepare the rest of the lasagne.

3. To prepare the béchamel, melt the 5 tablespoons of butter in a heavy-bottomed saucepan over low heat. Add the flour all at once and stir constantly until it is absorbed by the butter and cooked, about 2 minutes. Whisk in the milk and 1 1/2 cups of the fish broth. Add more fish broth until the sauce is loose, and cook, whisking constantly, until the sauce thickens. Add the anchovy fillets and cook until the anchovies have melted into the béchamel. Adjust the seasoning with salt and pepper to taste.

4. Heat 2 tablespoons of the olive oil and 4 tablespoons of butter in a large frying pan over medium heat. Add the garlic clove and sauté 1 or 2 minutes, until the garlic becomes fragrant but doesn't brown. Add half of the sliced zucchini. Turn the heat up to high and sauté for 4 to 5 minutes, just until it is a little soft. Remove the zucchini from the pan and set aside. Add the remaining olive oil and another 4 tablespoons of butter and repeat with the remaining zucchini.

5. Meanwhile, bring a large pot of water to a boil and place a clean dishtowel on your work surface or on a sheet pan. Add salt, a little bit of olive oil, and the lasagne, a few at a time so there is just 1 layer in the pot. Cook the pasta for only 1 minute. It will not be al dente, but remember it will cook more in the oven. Lift the lasagne out of the water and lay them in 1 layer on the towel. Repeat with the remaining lasagne.

Butter for greasing the baking dish
2 cups vegetable broth
4 fresh bay leaves
3/4 pound fresh cod fillets

FOR THE BÉCHAMEL
5 tablespoons unsalted butter
1/2 cup all-purpose flour
2 cups milk
1 1/2–2 cups reserved fish broth
8 anchovy fillets in olive oil
Salt and freshly ground black pepper

1/4 cup extra virgin olive oil
8 tablespoons (1 stick) unsalted butter, plus 3 tablespoons, cut into small pieces
1 garlic clove
2 pounds zucchini, cut into thin rounds
1 pound egg lasagne
1 cup freshly grated Parmesan cheese, plus more for the table

TIP When we layer the lasagne, we lay all the pasta pieces in one direction so that when you slice the lasagne, it looks pretty. We also tear the pieces of lasagne to fit the space we are trying to cover.

6. Place 1 layer of lasagne to cover the bottom of the buttered baking dish. Cover them with a third of the zucchini slices. Lift the cod out of the broth and break up a third of it over the zucchini slices. Pour one-fourth of the béchamel over the cod, using your fingers to spread it around. Sprinkle with Parmesan cheese. Repeat until all the ingredients are finished. The last layer will be just lasagne, béchamel, and Parmesan, with no zucchini or cod. Sprinkle the final layer with the small pieces of butter.

7. Place the lasagne in the oven to bake for 25 minutes, until it has a nice crust and is golden brown in places. Serve hot, dishing the lasagne out of the pan it was cooked in. Pass the Parmesan cheese.

When we buy fish at the market, we expect it to be absolutely fresh.

Classic Baked Lasagne
Lasagne Pasticciate Classiche

Serves 6

Lasagne was born in the north of Italy—Emilia, to be precise—but today it is a national dish. In the past, we always made the pasta by hand for lasagne, but now we buy it fresh or even use dried. And let us tell you a secret: in every good food shop, you can find good-quality, already-prepared fresh lasagne, or good-quality dried lasagne. You may not be the Queen of the Kitchen, but any time you make lasagne, you are a princess for sure.

1. Preheat the oven to 350°F. Butter a 13-×-9-inch baking dish.

2. Heat the olive oil in a large frying pan over medium heat. Add the onion and cook for 2 to 3 minutes, until it begins to soften. Turn the heat up to high, add the veal, and cook until the veal loses its pink color. Reduce the heat and add the broth, tomato sauce, carrots, sugar, and salt and pepper to taste. Add enough water (or broth) to cover and mix the ingredients well. Cover and simmer for about 45 minutes, stirring every 15 minutes or so and adding more water or broth if the pan becomes dry. Turn off the heat, discard the carrots, and adjust the salt, pepper, and sugar to taste. Pour the veal *ragù* into a large mixing bowl.

3. To make the béchamel, melt the 8 tablespoons of butter in a heavy-bottomed saucepan over low heat, being careful not to let it brown. Add the flour all at once, stirring constantly with a wooden spoon until the butter absorbs all the flour, about 2 minutes. Gradually pour in the milk, whisking constantly. Cook, still whisking constantly, until the sauce thickens. Add salt and pepper to taste. Raise the heat to medium and bring the béchamel to a low boil. Cook at a low boil for about 5 minutes, stirring constantly. Stir in the nutmeg and take the béchamel off the heat. If you have lumps, stir very quickly to remove. Pour the béchamel into the bowl with the veal *ragù* and stir to mix them together. When you are boiling the pasta, add a ladleful or more of hot pasta water to the ragù to loosen it.

4. Place a clean dishtowel on your work surface for draining the lasagne after they are cooked. Bring a large soup pot of water to a boil. Stir in a small fistful of salt and add the lasagne about 4 at a time—it's important that they don't touch in the pot—and cook until the pasta is al dente. Lift the lasagne out of the pot with a slotted spoon and lay them carefully in

Butter for greasing the baking dish
1/2 cup extra virgin olive oil
1 small white or yellow onion, chopped
1 pound ground veal
2 cups vegetable broth, more if needed
1/2 cup Fresh Tomato Sauce (page 9; or bottled sauce*)
1 large carrot, cut into four pieces
1 teaspoon sugar (or more to taste)
Salt and freshly ground black pepper

FOR THE BÉCHAMEL
8 tablespoons (1 stick) unsalted butter
2/3 cup all-purpose flour
4 cups milk
Salt and freshly ground black pepper
1/2 teaspoon freshly grated nutmeg

1 1/2 pounds fresh lasagne or 1 1/4 pounds dried lasagne
1 cup (about 3 ounces) freshly grated Parmesan cheese, plus more for passing at the table
A walnut of butter (about 2 tablespoons), cut into small pieces

See source list.

1 layer on the dishcloth. Cover with another damp dishcloth and continue until you have cooked all the lasagne.

5. Place a layer of lasagne over the bottom of the prepared baking dish. Rip the lasagne into smaller pieces to fit into the edges and corners. Spread a layer of the veal–béchamel sauce evenly over the lasagne and sprinkle with a light layer of grated Parmesan cheese. Continue until you have used all the ingredients. Scatter the butter pieces over the last layer.

6. Place the lasagne in the oven to bake for about 30 minutes, until the top is golden brown. Serve immediately in the same pan you cooked it in, with grated Parmesan at the table.

Parmesan is integral to our cooking—we grate it, shave it, and even boil the rind in soup.

Paolo's Pesto Lasagne
Lasagne con il Pesto del Cavaliere

Serves 4

Paolo is a man of pasta. Every night he makes pasta for his guests at the inn, and it seems every night it is a new invention. This one, with pesto, green beans, and cherry tomatoes, is a victory of summer, and one of his most brilliant creations. Incidentally, cavaliere literally means "the knighted one," and also refers to a gentleman.

1. Preheat the oven to 350°F. Grease a 13-×-11-inch baking dish with butter.

2. To prepare the béchamel, melt the 1/2 pound of butter in a large saucepan over medium heat. Add the flour all at once, stirring constantly until the butter has absorbed all the flour. Stir in 7 cups of the milk and bring to a low boil. Continue to cook it at a low boil, stirring constantly, for about 5 minutes to thicken. Add more milk if necessary for a loose béchamel. Stir in the nutmeg and salt and pepper to taste. Pour the béchamel into a large mixing bowl.

3. Warm 1/4 cup olive oil in a large frying pan over medium heat. Add the onions and sauté for about 3 minutes, until they are tender and slightly golden. Add the cherry tomatoes and salt and pepper to taste. Cover and cook until the tomatoes burst, about 5 minutes. Allow the tomatoes to cool to room temperature before adding them to the bowl with the béchamel.

4. To make the pesto, put the almonds, pine nuts, garlic, basil, and green beans in the bowl of a food processor fitted with a metal blade and puree. With the machine running on low speed, add 1/2 cup olive oil slowly through the feed tube. Add more oil if necessary to form a loose paste. Turn off the machine. Add salt and pepper to taste and blend again to incorporate the salt and pepper. Pour the pesto into the bowl with the béchamel and tomatoes.

5. Place a clean dry dishtowel on your work surface to lay the lasagne on after they're cooked. Bring a large saucepan of water to a boil. Stir in a small fistful of salt. Add the lasagne, about 4 at a time, depending on the size of the pot; you don't want the individual strips to touch. When the lasagne is al dente, carefully remove them from the boiling water and lay them on the towel to drain. Cover with a damp towel and con-

Butter for greasing the baking dish

FOR THE BÉCHAMEL
1/2 pound (2 sticks) unsalted butter
1 1/3 cups all-purpose flour
7 to 8 cups milk
1/2 teaspoon freshly grated nutmeg
Salt and freshly ground black pepper

1/4 cup extra virgin olive oil
1 small white or yellow onion, chopped
3/4 pound cherry tomatoes
Salt and freshly ground black peper

FOR THE PESTO
2 cups blanched almonds
1/2 cup pine nuts
4 garlic cloves
2 cups fresh basil leaves
1/2 pound green beans, boiled or steamed until just tender
1/2 cup (or more) extra virgin olive oil
Salt and freshly ground black pepper

1 1/2 pounds fresh or dried lasagne
1/2 cup freshly grated Parmesan cheese, plus more for passing at the table
A walnut of butter (about 2 tablespoons), cut into small pieces

tinue until all the lasagne is cooked. You may need more than 1 towel to lay them in 1 layer.

6. Place a layer of lasagne in the bottom of the prepared baking dish. Cover with a layer of the pesto–béchamel sauce and continue the layers ending with lasagne. Spread the sauce over the top layer, then sprinkle with the grated Parmesan cheese and the butter pieces. Place the lasagne in the oven to bake for about 30 minutes, until the top is golden brown. Serve hot in the same pan. Pass the Parmesan.

We use this basket to lift ingredients from the abbey entrance to our kitchen upstairs.

Orietta's Baked Penne Casserole with Leeks and Green Peas
Pasticcio di Penne al Forno di Orietta

Serves 4

This recipe comes from our friend Orietta, who with her sister, Antonella, owns a restaurant and inn, Villa Padura, in the nearby town of Castellana. The dish has eggs in it and then it's baked, so we think of it as a pasta casserole.

Butter for greasing the baking pan
1/2 cup extra virgin olive oil
2 leeks, cleaned and chopped (white part only)
1 red bell pepper, cored, seeded, and diced
6 ounces fresh or frozen green peas
Salt and freshly ground black pepper
3/4 pound penne
2 tablespoons finely chopped fresh Italian parsley
4 large eggs
1/3 cup (about 1 ounce) freshly grated Parmesan cheese, plus more for passing at the table
1/4 cup milk

... grease an 8-x-8-inch baking ...

... medium heat. Add the leeks ... begin to soften, 3 to 4 minutes. ... ons of hot water and cook for ... tender. Season with salt and ...

... water to a boil over high heat. ... ne and boil until the penne is ... ater and drain the pasta in a ... in the frying pan and place ... té for 1 minute, adding pasta ... ry. Add the parsley and mix ... cool to room temperature. ... ggs with the Parmesan cheese, ... e eggs to the cooled pasta and ... into the prepared baking pan. ... it even. Place the pan in the ... e crust is light golden brown. ... pasta rest for a few minutes. ... rve immediately with freshly

Barrington Area Library

Customer ID: 21487002075277

"Pasticcio means 'cake' or 'pie,' like something put in a pan and baked. But there is another meaning. You say, for instance, don't put anything else in a dish, otherwise it becomes like a pasticcio—a big mess!"

—G.

PENNE
was named after the ancestor of our modern pen: the quill. The fine point on each end of the pasta is like the end of the pen you dip in the ink. Penne rigate refers to that pasta shape with ridges on them. The ridges help to hold sauce on the pasta.

Maccheroni Gratinée with Olives and Tomatoes
Maccheroni con Pomodoro e Olive Gratinati

Serves 6

The olives we put in this pasta are from our own trees. We pick them in November. After that, the olives are sorted through one by one. Those that are perfect, with no blemishes and just the right size, we preserve for 2 or 3 months, until they are ready to eat. The others are for making olive oil.

1/3 cup extra virgin olive oil, plus more for greasing the baking pan
1 1/2 cups dry white wine
3/4 pound green olives, pitted and chopped
2 garlic cloves, minced
1/3 cup finely chopped fresh Italian parsley
1 cup Fresh Tomato Sauce (page 9; or bottled sauce*)
2 tablespoons heavy cream
Salt and freshly ground black pepper
1 pound maccheroni
1/4 pound fresh pecorino cheese (or provola), cubed
1/2 cup breadcrumbs

See source list.

1. Preheat the oven to 450°F. Grease an 8- or 9-inch round baking pan with olive oil.

2. Heat the wine in a large frying pan over low heat. Add the olives, garlic, and parsley and cook for 15 minutes, or until all the wine has evaporated and the pan is dry. Add the tomato sauce and cream and simmer on low heat for about 10 minutes. Adjust salt and pepper to taste.

3. Bring a saucepan of water to a boil. Add a small fistful of salt and the maccheroni and cook until the pasta is tender. Reserve a cupful of the pasta water and drain the pasta in a colander. Transfer the pasta to the pot with the olive mixture. Add the cubed pecorino and a splash of pasta water and toss, adding more pasta water until the pasta is wet and slippery.

4. Transfer the pasta into the prepared baking pan. Sprinkle with the breadcrumbs and drizzle the olive oil over the top. Place the pan in the oven and bake until the breadcrumbs are golden brown and crunchy, about 15 minutes. Serve very hot, with Parmesan on the table.

The word **MACCHERONI** likely comes from the root word *macar*, which means "happy" in either Greek or Arabic. I don't remember which language it is, but I do know that there is nobody happier than me in front of a dish of maccheroni. —G.

Cannelloni with Vegetable–Ricotta Filling
Cannelloni con Verdure e Ricotta

Serves 4

Cannelloni filled with Bolognese is the classic, but you can fill cannelloni with whatever you want. For this one, we made a filling of ricotta with potatoes and lettuce. When we don't have cannelloni, we use lasagne, rolled into cannelloni. If you do this, lay them snugly side by side in a baking pan so they can't roll open. There's no sauce to this recipe, but when it is baked, the ingredients inside the cannelloni melt together, making a rich and delicious dish.

1. Preheat the oven to 350°F. Butter a 9–×–13–inch baking dish.
2. Melt the butter and the oil in a large frying pan over low heat. Add the potatoes, onion, and 1/2 cup of water. Cover and simmer on low heat for about 15 minutes, or until the vegetables are almost tender, adding more water if the pan is dry. Add the lettuce and sauté until it wilts. Pass the vegetables through a food mill into a bowl. Add the fresh ricotta, and all but 3 tablespoons of the Parmesan and stir to mix. Season with salt and pepper to taste.
3. Bring a large saucepan of water to a boil. Stir in a small fistful of salt and a splash of oil. Add the cannelloni, only a few at once so they are not touching each other, and cook until al dente. Place them on a dish–towel to drain and repeat with the remaining cannelloni.
4. When the cannelloni are cool enough to touch, fill them with the vegetable–ricotta mixture. You can use a pastry bag to do this, or you can use a spoon to push the filling into the tube from both ends. Place the filled ravioli side by side in the baking dish. Brush the cannelloni with the melted butter. Mix the cream with the remaining 3 tablespoons of Parmesan and pour over the cannelloni. Bake for about 20 minutes, until the top is golden. Serve immediately in the same dish. Pass the Parmesan.

CANNELLONI
means "big cane," like a walking stick, or "pipe." This pasta is named for its shape, which is a large hollow tube, about the diameter of a cane. It is classically filled with veal, but you can use different ingredients if you want to get creative.

5 tablespoons unsalted butter, plus more for buttering the baking dish
2 tablespoons extra virgin olive oil
1 pound potatoes, peeled and thinly sliced
1 medium white or yellow onion, sliced
1 head butter lettuce (or any tender lettuce), washed, cored, and thinly sliced
6 ounces fresh ricotta, drained in a colander for 1 hour
1/2 cup (about 1 1/2 ounces) freshly grated Parmesan cheese, plus more for the table
Salt and freshly ground black pepper
10 ounces cannelloni
Soybean oil (or other mild–flavored oil) for the pasta water
4 tablespoons (1/2 stick) unsalted butter, melted
1 cup heavy cream

OPPOSITE: *In Sicily, we grow many varieties of olives.*

FOR THE RAGÙ DI TRITATO

1 cup extra virgin olive oil
1 medium white or yellow onion,
  finely chopped
2 1/2 pounds ground veal
1 cup tomato paste
One 6-ounce piece Parmesan
  cheese rind
2 carrots, cut into four pieces
1 heaping tablespoon sugar
  (or more to taste)
2 cups vegetable broth
Salt and freshly ground black pepper

Breadcrumbs (for dusting the
  baking pan)
Salt
2 pounds anelletti

FOR THE BÉCHAMEL

8 tablespoons (1 stick) unsalted butter
2/3 cup all-purpose flour
4 cups milk
1/4 teaspoon freshly grated nutmeg
Salt and freshly ground black pepper

3 Polpette alla Wanda (meatballs,
  recipe follows)
4 cups Fresh Tomato Sauce (page 9; or
  bottled sauce*)
2 cups frozen or fresh green peas,
  cooked to tender
1/2 pound prosciutto cotto (cooked
  ham), coarsely chopped
1 cup provolone, diced (about 4
  ounces)
1/2 cup (about 1 1/2 ounces) freshly
  grated pecorino cheese
1/2 cup (about 1 1/2 ounces) freshly
  grated Parmesan cheese, plus more
  for the table
4 tablespoons (1/2 stick) unsalted
  butter, softened
Freshly grated black pepper

See source list.

Baked Timballo of Anelletti with Veal and Vegetables
Anelletti al Forno

Serves 12 to 14

This is the most classic timballo in Sicily. You'll find it at lunchtime in little bars and cafés all around Sicily, either sliced like a cake or made in individual baking pans. We make it at home, but only for special occasions, because with the meatballs and the ragù, it takes a lot of time to prepare. If you feel like embarking on a cooking project on a weekend afternoon, this is the perfect thing. A timballo always justifies the effort. This one can be prepared up to a day in advance. Keep it in the pan, and when you're ready to serve it, put it in a 300°F oven until it is warm.

1. To prepare the *ragù*, heat the olive oil over medium-high heat. Add the onion and sauté for 3 to 4 minutes, until it is tender and beginning to color. Add the veal and sauté, stirring often and breaking up the meat as it cooks, until it loses its pink color. Stir in the tomato paste, Parmesan rind, carrots, sugar, and broth and bring it to a boil. Reduce the heat and simmer for about 1 1/2 hours, adding water if the pan becomes dry and stirring occasionally until you have a rich, thick *ragù*. Discard the carrots and adjust salt, pepper, and sugar to taste.

2. Preheat the oven to 450°F. Grease a 12- or 14-inch round baking pan with butter and dust it with breadcrumbs, tapping out any excess crumbs.

3. Bring a large soup pot of water to a boil. Stir in a fistful of salt and the anelletti and cook until the pasta is tender. Reserve a cupful of the pasta water, drain the pasta quickly in a colander, and return it to the pot you cooked it in.

4. To prepare the béchamel, melt the butter in a small saucepan over medium heat. Add the flour all at once, stirring constantly until the butter has absorbed all the flour and the flour cooks, about 2 minutes. Whisk in 3 1/2 cups of the milk. Increase the heat, bring mixture to a low boil, and continue to cook, whisking constantly, for about 5 minutes to thicken. Add more milk if necessary to make a loose béchamel. Stir in the nutmeg and salt and pepper to taste.

5. Crush the meatballs into a large bowl. Add the *ragù*, tomato sauce, peas, prosciutto cotto, provolone, pecorino, Parmesan, butter, pepper to taste, and the béchamel and stir thoroughly but gently until all the ingredients are combined. Add hot pasta water, if necessary, to give it a loose, slippery consistency.

6. Spoon the pasta in a layer into the baking pan. Smooth it out so that it is even and press down to pack it slightly.

7. Place the timballo in the oven and bake for 30 minutes, or until the top is golden brown. Remove the timballo from the oven and let it rest for at least 5 minutes. Run a knife around the edge of the pan. Place a round serving platter 4 to 6 inches larger than the baking pan over the pan. Quickly invert the dish and gently lift off the pan. Serve warm. Pass the Parmesan.

ANELLETTI
are small, ring–shaped pasta. If you can't find them for this, substitute rigatoni. They are not at all similar, but we Sicilians are creatures of our habits and traditions, and it is for one or the other that rigatoni is what we use whenever we don't have anelletti.

"My mamma is great at flipping the timballo. She puts the pan and the platter on her head and flips it at the same time she bends down and lowers the timballo to the table."
—G.

FLIPPING THE TIMBALLO
To remove the timballo from the pan, first slide a small knife around the edges to loosen up any bits that might be sticking. Cover the pan with a platter a few inches bigger than the pan. Lift up both the timballo and the platter together and quickly flip the timballo over while bringing it down onto the counter.

Wanda's Veal and Pork Meatballs
Polpette alla Wanda

Serves 8

We Italians do not have the same custom of eating spaghetti with meatballs that you do in America. We eat meatballs as a main course, a meat dish. But if we have any leftover meatballs, we do have them with pasta, crumbled over a plate of spaghetti with tomato sauce. Meatballs are also integral to the anelletti al forno, *our great Sicilian timballo.*

1 pound ground veal
1 1/2 pounds ground pork
2 large eggs
1/3 cup finely chopped fresh Italian parsley
1/3 cup (about 1 ounce) freshly grated pecorino cheese
3/4 cup day-old bread, soaked in water and squeezed dry
1/4 pound mortadella, diced
1/4 pound prosciutto cotto (cooked ham), diced
Extra virgin olive oil
1 medium onion, finely chopped
1/3 cup tomato paste
1 tablespoon sugar (or more to taste)
Salt and freshly ground black pepper
All-purpose flour

1. In a large bowl, combine the veal, pork, eggs, parsley, pecorino, bread, mortadella, and prosciutto cotto and knead with your hands to mix thoroughly. Form into 8 large balls and flatten into a slightly oval shape.
2. Pour enough oil into a large frying pan to fill to 1/4 inch and heat over medium–high heat. Fry the meatballs until they are brown on all sides. Transfer them to a heavy pot.
3. Add the onion, tomato paste, sugar, and 1 cup of water to the frying pan you cooked the meatballs in, scraping to release any bits sticking to the pan. Cook for about 4 minutes and season with salt, pepper, and more sugar to taste. Pour the sauce over the meatballs. Sprinkle with flour and add enough water to cover. Put a lid on the pot and simmer the meatballs over low heat for 1 hour, adding more water if the sauce is sticking to the pot, until they are cooked through.

"The Leopard's Timballo"
Timballo alla Gattopardo

Serves 8

The novel Il Gattopardo—The Leopard—is the masterpiece of Sicilian literature. The author, Giuseppe di Lampedusa, characterizes Sicilians in such a way that we all recognize ourselves in his description. The story shows the way of life of the Sicilian aristocracy before Sicily became connected to Italy, and during the transition when that connection was made. One of the best-known passages from this book is when the Leopard, who is a prince, says: "We need everything to change so that everything can remain the same." This timballo is served in the novel during a lunch in the house of the prince; there is such a sensual description of the smooth golden crust, the knife cutting through it as if it were butter, and the steam that rises, rich with the scents of liver and cinnamon. This recipe is the rendition of that fictional timballo that Mary Taylor Simeti, the historian and Sicilian cookbook author, replicated based on that description. She was kind enough to share it with us for this book.

1. Preheat the oven to 350°F. Smear an 8-inch round baking pan with butter. Dust the pan with flour and tap the excess flour out into the sink.
2. Heat the oil in a large frying pan over medium heat. Add the onion and sauté for 3 to 5 minutes, until it becomes soft and translucent. Add the chicken and sauté until it is golden brown on all sides. Pour the Marsala into the pan and allow to cook for 1 minute, to evaporate the alcohol, then pour the porcini and the soaking water into the frying pan over the chicken. Lower the heat and sauté the *ragù* for 10 minutes, stirring occasionally so the chicken doesn't stick to the bottom of the pan. Add more water if the pan is so dry that the meat continues to stick.
3. Add the *estratto*, chopped chicken livers, prosciutto cotto, and 4 tablespoons of the butter. Stir so that the ingredients are combined and sauté for 2 to 3 minutes, until the chicken livers are cooked through.
4. Meanwhile, bring a large saucepan of water to boil. Stir in a small fistful of salt, add the rigatoni, and cook until the pasta is just al dente; you should feel the pasta on your teeth when you bite into it. Save a large cupful of the pasta water, then drain the rigatoni in a colander.
5. Put the rigatoni back in the pot you cooked it in and place over medium-high heat. Add some of the *ragù* and about 1/2 cup of the reserved pasta water and stir so that the *condimento* coats the rigatoni. Stir in the remaining *ragù*, the remaining butter, salt and pepper to taste,

8 tablespoons (1 stick) unsalted butter, plus more for greasing the baking pan
All-purpose flour for dusting the baking pan and rolling out the pastry dough
1 cup extra virgin olive oil
1 small white or yellow onion, finely chopped
1/2 pound skinless, boneless chicken breast, cut into 1/2-inch cubes
1/2 cup dry Marsala
3 ounces dried porcini mushrooms, broken into small pieces and soaked in hot water for 20 minutes
2 cups Estratto di Carne (recipe follows)
10 ounces chicken livers, chopped
1/2 pound prosciutto cotto (cooked ham), chopped
Salt
1 pound rigatoni
Freshly ground black pepper
1/4 cup freshly grated Parmesan cheese, plus more for passing at the table
1 recipe Savory Pastry Dough (recipe follows)
1 egg white, lightly beaten

"There are really two kinds of kitchens in Sicily. There is the kitchen of what you call the Mediterranean diet, which is the diet of peasants: pasta, tomato sauce, chickpeas. And there is the aristocratic kitchen, which has lots of meat in the diet, cream, béchamel, and pasta en crosta, like the timballo alla Gattopardo."

—G.

and the grated Parmesan. Add more pasta water if necessary; it's important that the rigatoni be very moist and slippery before you put it in the oven so that the baked timballo does not turn out dry.

6. Remove the pastry dough from the refrigerator. Sprinkle flour on your work surface and place one of the balls in the center. Dust a rolling pin with flour and roll the dough out to about 1 foot in diameter. It should be about 1/4 to 1/3 inch thick. Fold the dough in half to pick it up. Place the dough in the greased and floured baking pan and use your fingers to press the dough into the creases of the pan. Roll out the other round of dough to the same size, adding more flour to your work surface and your rolling pin so the dough doesn't stick.

7. Pour the rigatoni into the baking pan on top of the dough, making sure to scrape out all the juices with a spatula or with your hand. Place the second pastry dough round on top of the rigatoni. Seal the bottom and top crusts together well by pinching them with your fingers. Poke a few holes in the top crust with a fork to let out the steam that develops inside the timballo (otherwise you will have an explosion in your oven).

8. Brush the crust with the beaten egg white. Place the timballo in the oven to bake for about 30 minutes, until the crust is golden. Remove the pan from the oven and allow the timballo to rest for 5 to 10 minutes. Turn the timballo out onto a serving dish, slice, and serve very hot with Parmesan cheese at the table.

Estratto di Carne

Makes about 2 cups

The estratto di carne for this recipe can be prepared a day or two in advance. Estratto means extract—what you are using is only the sauce that comes from braising the veal with the vegetables. It might seem awkward to make an entire veal roast just to have the sauce from cooking it, but this is the way it's done. If you substitute broth, it's not as rich, and the timballo just won't be the same. My granny used to make an entire veal roast just to toss the estratto with pasta, like sedanini or pennette. She would then serve the veal roast cold with either mayonnaise or a green sauce of capers, chopped parsley, olive oil, salt, and pepper, all chopped fine and smashed together with a fork. —G.

1. Heat the oil over high heat in a deep oval or rectangular casserole dish as close to the shape of the veal as possible. Place the meat in the dish and brown it on all sides. Add the butter, carrots, onion, potatoes, rosemary, celery stalks, salt and pepper, and enough water to almost cover the veal. Sprinkle the top of the veal with the flour and bring the water to a boil over high heat. Reduce the heat and simmer, partially covered, for 2 to 2 1/2 hours, turning the meat occasionally. To test the meat for doneness, insert a long fork into the center of the roast. When no blood comes out and the fork goes in very easily, the veal is done.

2. Remove the meat from the liquid and reserve for another use. For this recipe you want only the *estratto*, the juices from the veal. Pass the liquid and vegetables from the pan through a food mill. You need at least 2 cups of juices for the timballo. If you do not have 2 cups, add water to the *estratto*.

TIP When you are making baked pasta, remember that the pasta will continue to cook when you put the dish in the oven. So you want to make sure not to overcook the pasta in the water. You want it just al dente, not tender.

1 cup extra virgin olive oil
One 3-pound boneless veal roast, tied
2 tablespoons (1/4 stick) unsalted butter
2 carrots, sliced into 1/2-inch rounds
1 large red onion, chopped
2 small potatoes, peeled and cut into quarters
2 tablespoons finely chopped fresh rosemary
2 celery stalks
Salt and freshly ground black pepper
1/4 cup all-purpose flour

Savory Pastry Dough

My mother rolls out pastry dough with a rolling pin. To do it this way, use the pan to measure so that you roll the dough out to fit the bottom and the sides. I like to press on the dough with my hands until it is flat. Then I piece together the dough pieces on the bottom of the pan like a mosaic. I find this process more amusing. Plus, when you do it this way, the crust, when you flip it over, looks more rustic. I think it's nice to see the seams, the sign of the single pieces put together. They are like a drawing on top of the timballo. There is not a doubt that it is homemade. You can bake any timballo using this crust to make it very special and festive. This dough also freezes well for future use. If you like this timballo, double the recipe so you'll have the dough ready for the next time you want to make it.

4 cups all–purpose flour
1 1/4 cups sugar
2 teaspoons salt
2 teaspoons ground cinnamon
2 tablespoons baking powder
6 large eggs at room temperature,
  lightly beaten
3/4 pound (3 sticks) unsalted butter,
  melted and cooled to room
  temperature

1. Stir the flour, sugar, salt, cinnamon, and baking powder together in a medium bowl. Add the eggs and mix them into the flour with a pastry cutter or the blades of 2 knives. Gradually pour in the butter, using the pastry cutter or knives to cut it into the flour. (To make this dough using a food processor, put your dry ingredients into the bowl of the food processor fitted with a metal blade. Add the butter all at once and use the pulse button to cut the butter into the flour until it is a coarse crumb consistency. Then dump it out onto the work surface and proceed.)

2. Turn the dough out of the bowl and onto a clean, flat work surface. Dust your hands with flour, then knead the dough just enough to make it stick together. Take care not to overwork the dough or you will have a tough crust.

3. Form the dough into 2 balls, cover them with plastic wrap, and refrigerate them for at least 1 hour or overnight.

Veal Timballo with an Eggplant "Shell"
Timballo Foderato di Melanzane

Serves 8

Our friends and regular visitors Carlo and Giorgina, from San Francisco, cook often from our books. They especially like the recipe for a timballo covered in eggplant and filled with meat. They asked us to create a pasta timballo using eggplant on the outside. We did, and this is it! It is a very dramatic dish to present at the table.

1. Preheat the oven to 350°F.
2. Pour enough olive oil into a large skillet to fill to 1 inch. Heat over medium–high heat and add the eggplant slices in 1 layer to fry until golden brown, turning once. Drain on paper towels and repeat with the remaining eggplant.
3. To make the tomato sauce, heat 1/2 cup of the olive oil in a large frying pan over medium heat. Add the garlic and sauté for 1 minute, stirring constantly to avoid browning. Add the tomatoes, adjust salt to taste, and cook on medium heat for 10 minutes. Add the basil leaves and turn off the heat.
4. Heat remaining 1/2 cup of olive oil in a large frying pan. Add the onion and sauté until it begins to soften, about 5 minutes. Add the pancetta and sauté until it is golden brown, about 2 minutes. Add the ground veal, 2 tablespoons water, and salt and pepper to taste and cook until the veal is golden brown.
5. Bring a big saucepan of water to a boil. Stir in a small fistful of salt and the penne and boil until the penne is al dente. Reserve a cupful of pasta water and drain quickly in a colander. Transfer the drained penne to a large mixing bowl. Add the tomato sauce and a splash of pasta water for consistency, and toss.
6. While the pasta is cooking, liberally grease a 10–inch round or oval baking dish with oil. Line the bottom and sides with the fried eggplant slices, reserving enough eggplant to cover the finished timballo.
7. Spoon a third of the pasta in the bottom of the baking pan. Cover with a third of the ground veal. Top with a third of the mozzarella slices and sprinkle with grated Parmesan cheese. Repeat in 2 more layers. Top with a layer of the eggplant slices and place in the oven to bake 40 minutes. Remove from the oven and wait 5 minutes before turning the pasta out onto a serving platter. Slice and serve and pass the Parmesan.

1 cup extra virgin olive oil, plus more for greasing the baking pan and frying the eggplant

2 pounds eggplant, thinly sliced lengthwise

2 garlic cloves, minced

One 28–ounce can peeled whole tomatoes, drained in a colander and broken up with your hands

Salt

5 fresh basil leaves

1 small white or yellow onion, diced

2 ounces pancetta (or bacon), cut into 1/2–inch cubes

10 ounces ground veal

Freshly ground black pepper

1 pound penne

1/2 pound fresh mozzarella, thinly sliced

1 cup (about 3 ounces) freshly grated Parmesan cheese, plus more to pass at the table

Eggplant and Ziti Timballo
Timballo di Melanzane e Ziti

Serves 8

Pasta with eggplant and tomato is a classic for us. We put this in a timballo to make it more festive. In Sicily, our eggplants don't have the bitterness of much of the eggplant we tasted in America. If you buy tender young eggplant, it most likely will not be bitter. But if you think your eggplant might be bitter (if it has a lot of seeds, this is likely), you may want to salt the eggplant slices and let them "sweat" in a colander before frying it.

8 tablespoons (1 stick) unsalted butter, plus more for greasing the timballo pan

Breadcrumbs for dusting the timballo pan (about 1/4 cup)

Soybean oil (or other mild-flavored oil) for frying the eggplant

5 medium eggplants, sliced 1/2-inch thick

A *ciuffo* (bunch) of whole fresh basil leaves (about 15 leaves)

1/2 cup extra virgin olive oil, plus more for the pasta water

2 garlic cloves

1 small white or yellow onion

One 28-ounce can peeled whole tomatoes, drained in a colander and broken up with your fingers

Salt and freshly ground black pepper

1 tablespoon sugar (or more to taste)

1 pound ziti (broken into 3 pieces if long)

4 ounces (about 1 cup) caciocavallo cheese, shredded (or provolone)

3 eggs, hard-boiled and peeled

Freshly grated Parmesan cheese

1. Grease a 12-inch round baking dish or cake pan with butter and dust with breadcrumbs.

2. Pour enough oil into a large frying pan so that it is 1 inch deep. Heat the oil over medium-high heat until it sizzles when you drop water in it but is not smoking. Lay the eggplant slices in 1 layer and fry, turning them once, until both sides are golden brown. Have a colander nearby on top of a bowl or in the sink. Place the cooked eggplant in the colander to drain off as much of the grease as possible. Repeat until you have fried all the eggplant slices. When they have cooled slightly, toss all but 5 of the whole basil leaves in the colander with the eggplant.

3. Preheat the oven to 350°F.

4. Heat the olive oil with the garlic cloves and the whole onion in a saucepan over medium heat and sauté until the garlic and onion are light golden brown. Remove the garlic and onion from the oil and discard. Add the tomatoes, salt and pepper to taste, sugar, and the remaining basil leaves and cook for 10 minutes. Taste to make sure you have enough salt and sugar and add more if desired.

5. Meanwhile, bring a large saucepan of water to a boil. Stir in a small fistful of salt and the ziti and boil until the pasta is al dente. Reserve a cupful of the pasta water and drain the pasta quickly in a colander. Return the pasta to the pot you cooked it in. Add half of the tomato sauce, the butter, a splash of pasta water (about 1/4 cup), and half of the shredded cheese and stir. Add more pasta water if the pasta looks dry and the sauce is not coating it easily.

6. While the pasta is cooking, lay half of the fried eggplant slices in 1 layer in the prepared baking pan. Place half of the tossed pasta on top of the first layer of eggplant. Drizzle the pasta with a little more sauce and

sprinkle with a thin layer of caciocavallo cheese. Place the remaining eggplant in another layer and add the remaining pasta and sauce. The last layer does not have any cheese.

7. Place the timballo in the oven to bake for 20 minutes, or until the ziti has a nice golden crust. Don't overcook the timballo or it will dry out. Remove the timballo from the oven and allow it to cool for a few minutes before removing it from the pan.

8. Remove the timballo. Cut the hard-boiled eggs into quarters and arrange them upright like little spikes around the edges of the timballo. Serve warm with freshly grated Parmesan on the table.

TIP A little secret we have for peeling eggs is to first break a small hole in the small end of the egg. Then put the hole to your mouth and blow into it. This gets air between the egg and the shell and makes it easier to peel. Maybe it's just an old wives' tale, but we believe it works.

"To nourish with good food is a sort of nourishment for the mind, not only for the stomach."

—G.

Capellini Timballo with Peas, Edam, and Ham
Timballo di Capellini

Serves 8

TIP After making a béchamel, if it is still very lumpy and you are very desperate, you can pass it through a food mill. This shouldn't happen, but if it does, this is the way to fix it.

2 tablespoons (1/4 stick) butter, plus more for greasing the baking pan
Breadcrumbs for dusting the baking pan (about 1/2 cup)
1/2 onion, diced
1/4 pound frozen green peas

FOR THE BÉCHAMEL
6 tablespoons (3/4 stick) unsalted butter
2/3 cup all-purpose flour
3–4 cups whole milk
Salt and freshly ground black pepper
1/4 teaspoon freshly grated nutmeg

Soybean oil (or other mild-flavored oil) for the pasta water
1 pound capellini
1 cup (about 3 ounces) freshly grated Parmesan cheese, plus more for the table
1/2 cup breadcrumbs
3 tablespoons unsalted butter, cut into small pieces

This is a recipe that our friend Ginevra gave us. It is the masterpiece of her cooking. She's a good cook, but she doesn't cook often, and she doesn't make many dishes. Every time she has a big dinner, she prepares this pasta. We all know, and above all she knows, that it will be a success. With this, you can make one big timballo or many small timballini. Made in timballini, this pasta is very popular for wedding parties, because it's elegant and can be prepared in advance.

1. Preheat the oven to 450°F. Grease a large round baking dish (10 or 12 inches) liberally with butter and sprinkle with breadcrumbs. Turn the pan over a sink to discard any excess crumbs.
2. Melt the butter in a large frying pan with 2 tablespoons of water. Add the onion and cook until soft and translucent, about 10 minutes. Add the peas and cook about 10 minutes more, until they are tender.
3. To make the béchamel, melt the butter in a heavy-bottomed saucepan over low heat, being careful not to let it brown. Add the flour all at once, stirring constantly with a wooden spoon until the butter absorbs all the flour and the flour cooks, about 2 minutes. Gradually pour in 3 cups of the milk, stirring constantly. Raise the heat and bring the béchamel to a low boil. Cook the béchamel at a low boil for about 5 minutes, stirring constantly, until it is thick. Add more milk if necessary to make a loose béchamel. Take the béchamel off the heat and season with salt, pepper, and nutmeg. If it has lumps, stir very quickly to remove the lumps. Stir in peas and onions.
4. Meanwhile, bring a large saucepan to a boil over high heat. Stir in a small fistful of salt and a splash of oil. Break the capellini in half into the water and use a pasta fork to stir it well. When the water returns to a boil, cook the capellini for just about 1 more minute, until it is just tender but not mushy. With a spaghetti strainer, lift the pasta out of the water and into a large bowl. As you put the pasta in the bowl, add the béchamel and 1/2 cup of the Parmesan cheese in layers. Toss the capellini with the béchamel, adding enough pasta water so it is slippery and the strands do not stick together. If the pasta is at all dry, it will be very dry after it is baked.

5. Transfer the pasta to the prepared baking dish. Press the capellini down with a large spoon or your hands. Mix the breadcrumbs and the remaining 1/2 cup of Parmesan in a small bowl and sprinkle over the top with the butter pieces, and bake until it has a golden brown crust, about 40 minutes. Turn the pasta out of the pan and serve warm, sliced, with grated Parmesan cheese on the table.

"Only after you're done pressing down on the pasta can you lick your fingers."

—W.

Peter's Timballo of Winter Squash and Sausages
Il Preferito di Peter con Zucca e Salsiccia

Serves 8

Paolo is very adventurous in the kitchen. He loves making pasta and is always inventing new pastas to serve at his albergo at Gangivecchio. Timballos are his specialty. He made this one for our editor, Peter Gethers, and Peter made us promise to include it in the book. Paolo uses crushed almond biscotti in place of breadcrumbs for dusting the timballo pan, something I'm sure he invented just for this dish. If you do not want to make a timballo, toss the condimento *with rigatoni and serve the pasta dusted with the crushed almond biscotti mixed with grated Parmesan cheese.*

1 cup extra virgin olive oil, plus more
  for the pasta water
8 tablespoons (1 stick) unsalted
  butter, plus more for greasing the
  baking pan
1 small white or yellow onion, diced
3 garlic cloves, minced
1 cup dry white wine
1 pound Italian sausage, removed
  from casings
1 pound winter squash, peeled and
  cut into 1-inch cubes
1 cup vegetable broth
1 cup Fresh Tomato Sauce (page 9; or
  bottled sauce*)
Salt and freshly ground black pepper

FOR THE BÉCHAMEL
8 tablespoons (1 stick) unsalted butter
2/3 cup all-purpose flour
3–4 cups milk
A few gratings freshly grated nutmeg
  (or a pinch of ground nutmeg)
Salt and freshly ground black pepper

1 pound tagliatelle
5 to 7 almond biscotti, crushed to
  coarse crumbs
Freshly grated Parmesan cheese

*See source list.

1. Preheat the oven to 400°F.

2. Warm the oil and butter together in a large frying pan over medium heat. Add the onion and sauté for a few minutes until it begins to soften. Add the garlic and sauté a few minutes more, until it is light golden brown and fragrant. Pour the wine in the skillet and simmer until it has turned the onions light brown, about 5 minutes. Add the sausage and use a wooden spoon or spatula to break it into pieces. Cook the sausage until it is golden brown and cooked through. Add the cubed squash, vegetable broth, and tomato sauce and simmer until the squash is very tender. Season with salt and pepper to taste.

3. To prepare the béchamel, melt the butter in a large saucepan over medium heat. Add the flour all at once, stirring constantly until the butter has absorbed all the flour and the flour cooks, about 2 minutes. Whisk in 3 cups of the milk. Increase the heat and bring it to a low boil. Continue to cook it at a low boil, whisking constantly, for about 5 minutes to thicken. Add more milk if necessary to make a loose béchamel. Stir in the nutmeg and adjust salt and pepper to taste. Pour the béchamel into the pan with the *condimento*. Taste again for salt. Keep the *condimento* warm over very low heat.

4. Meanwhile, bring a large saucepan of water to a boil. Stir in a small fistful of salt and a splash of olive oil. Add the tagliatelle and cook, stirring occasionally, until the pasta is al dente.

5. While the pasta is cooking, grease a 9- or 10-inch round baking pan with butter. Dust it with some of the crushed almond biscotti, tapping out any excess crumbs but reserving them to top the timballo.

6. Reserve 1 cup of *condimento* from the pan. When the tagliatelle is done, lift it out of the pasta water and into the pan with the *condimento* and a splash of pasta water. Stir the pasta with the *condimento* over high heat for 2 to 3 minutes, adding more pasta water as needed to keep the pasta from being dry or sticky.

7. Transfer the pasta to the prepared timballo pan. Press down lightly to make it level. Sprinkle with the remaining biscotti crumbs and put the timballo in the oven to bake for about 20 minutes, until the top is golden brown. Remove the timballo from the oven and let it rest for about 5 minutes before turning it out onto a serving platter. Serve hot, topped with a spoonful of the reserved *condimento*. Pass the Parmesan cheese.

Ragù Timballo for a Picnic in the Country
Timballo di Ziti per una Scampagnata

Serves 10

In the summertime we often have guests who want to take a hike and have lunch in the country. We carry this in our Jeep and meet them at the picnic spot, where we lay a table-cloth on the grass and serve this pasta as a main course.

1/2 pound (2 sticks) unsalted butter

1 1/4 cups extra virgin olive oil, plus more for the pasta water and for greasing the pan

1 medium white or yellow onion, halved and sliced thin

1 pound skinless, boneless chicken breast, chopped into 1/2–inch pieces

2 pounds ground beef

2 pounds ground pork

1/2 cup *estratto** (or tomato paste)

1 cup red wine

1 tablespoon sugar (or more to taste)

Salt and freshly ground black pepper

1 small *ciuffo* (bunch) fresh basil leaves

3 pounds ziti (broken in three parts if long)

1/2 cup breadcrumbs

1/2 cup grated pecorino cheese

1/2 cup grated Parmesan cheese, plus more for dusting the timballo

1/2 pound cubed caciocavallo cheese (or provolone)

*See source list.

1. Preheat the oven to 450°F.

2. Melt the butter, 1 cup of olive oil, and a couple of spoonfuls of water in a large saucepan over medium heat. Add the onion slices and sauté them for about 10 minutes, until they are tender and golden.

3. Turn the heat to high, add the meats to the pot, and sauté until they are brown on the outside and just cooked through, about 5 minutes. Add the *estratto* and enough water so that the meat doesn't stick to the pan. Lower the heat to medium and cook for 10 minutes, until the meat has absorbed all the liquid. Add the wine and cook until it evaporates. Season with sugar, salt, and pepper to taste. Add the basil leaves and a few more spoonfuls of water to the pot and let the sauce simmer for 10 to 15 minutes, stirring from time to time, until you have a rich, dark brown *ragù*. Once the meat is nice and brown, add a cup or two of water, enough so that your *ragù* has a nice gravy, no thinner than tomato sauce.

4. Meanwhile, bring a very large soup or pasta pot of water to a boil. Stir in a small fistful of salt, a splash of olive oil, and the ziti, and cook the pasta until it is al dente. Reserve a large cupful of the pasta water and drain the ziti quickly in a colander.

5. While the pasta is cooking, prepare your timballo pan. Coat the bottom and sides with olive oil, then sprinkle it with breadcrumbs; shake them around so they cover the pan, and toss out the excess crumbs.

6. Put a quarter of the drained ziti back into the pot you cooked it in. Add some *ragù* and a splash of pasta water and toss it with the ziti. Add some more pasta, some more *ragù*, and a little more pasta water and toss again. Stir in all the cheeses. Continue adding the ziti and *ragù* and a little pasta water until everything is mixed together.

7. Spread the pasta into the prepared timballo pan. Press the pasta down with a wooden spoon or with your hands to make it more compact. Dust the top with more breadcrumbs passed through a sieve first to make them very fine. Finally dust the timballo with a light sprinkling of Parmesan. (You can make the timballo up to this point a day ahead of time.) Place the timballo in the oven and bake it for 25 to 30 minutes, until it has a light golden crust. Take it out of the oven and let it cool. Run a knife along the edges of the pan to release any sticking bits.

8. Place a serving platter that's at least 4 inches wider than the timballo over the pan. Quickly invert the pan and platter and remove the baking pan. Let the timballo rest for a few minutes before serving it. Serve hot, with freshly grated Parmesan. And don't eat anything else.

ZITI

is a long, hollow tube–shaped pasta. It is the big daddy of bucatini and maccheroncini, and is the same inconvenience to eat. If you eat it in all its length, it is absolutely dangerous for your table neighbor. We suggest breaking it in at least 2 parts before cooking. We always break it—usually in 3 parts—for a timballo. But in America, it seems the manufacturer has done the job of breaking the ziti for you.

SPECIALTY SOURCES

For sliced meats, like prosciutto, pancetta, and speck, and for cheeses like ricotta, mozzarella, and provola, try your local Italian specialty store or gourmet market.

The people behind the following shops dedicate their lives to sourcing regional artisanal products and are a great source for things like salt-packed capers, *bottarga*, dried beans, canned tomatoes, simple tomato sauce, *estratto*, and unusual pasta shapes. If you can't find the specific pasta shape called for in a recipe, choose one with the same qualities: a ridged pasta if that is what is called for, or a tubular one, a long or short one, and so on.

BAY CITIES ITALIAN DELI
1517 Lincoln Boulevard
Santa Monica, CA 90401
(310) 395-8279

A. G. FERRARI FOODS
Has many Bay Area locations
www.agferrari.com

FORMAGGIO KITCHEN
244 Huron Avenue
Cambridge, MA 02138
(617) 354-4750

268 Shawmut Avenue
Boston, MA 02118
(617) 350-6996
(888) 212-3224

www.formaggiokitchen.com

ITALIAN FOOD CENTER
186 Grand Street
New York, NY 10013
(212) 925-2954

MURRAY'S CHEESE SHOP
257 Bleecker Street
New York, NY 10014
(212) 922-1540
www.murrayscheese.com

THE PASTA SHOP
1786 Fourth Street
Berkeley, CA 94710
(510) 528-1786

ZINGERMAN'S
(888) 636-8162
www.zingermans.com

THERE EXISTS

Soft melancholy exists, full of unknown regrets
that have the taste of summer afternoons
on Sicilian mountainsides

by stone houses with dogs sleeping in the sun,
and strangled calls of irritable old cocks, whilst
a hot wind wraps and deadens the song of
antique bells . . .

a dull humming of busy flies,
trickles of dripping water
where bony cows, in slowly drinking,
see reflected liquid thoughtful glances.

—Wanda Tornabene

INDEX

A

Agrigento-style garlic and oil spaghetti with saffron, 32

Alda's pastasciutta with green beans and pecorino, 28

almonds:
casareccia with Gangivecchio's five-nut pesto, 51
Giovanna's lasagnette with creamy tomato sauce, toasted almonds, and pecorino cheese, 46

anchovies:
fiery spaghetti with anchovies, olives, and capers in a quick tomato sauce, 20
pink spaghetti with anchovies and breadcrumbs, 37
quick spicy pennette with anchovies and buffalo mozzarella, 16

anelletti, 147
baked timballo of anelletti with veal and vegetables, 146–7

apple:
tagliolini with green apple pesto and speck, 34

artichoke(s):
farfalle with artichoke hearts, fava beans, and peas, 86
Orietta's linguine with shrimp and fried artichokes, 92

arugula:
cavatelli with arugula and pecorino, 35
Paolo's arugula pesto the Chez Panisse way, 50

asparagus:
pappardelle with asparagus, walnuts, and speck, 72

B

baked pastas and timballos, 132–61
baked orecchiette with lamb ragù and melted mozzarella, 136
baked timballo of anelletti with veal and vegetables, 146–7
cannelloni with vegetable-ricotta filling, 145
capellini timballo with peas, edam, and ham, 156–7
classic baked lasagna, 139–40
eggplant and ziti timballo, 154–5
fresh cod and zucchini lasagna, 137–8
"The Leopard's timballo," 149–50
maccheroni gratinée with olives and tomatoes, 144
Orietta's baked penne casserole with leeks and green peas, 143
Paolo's pesto lasagna, 141–2
Peter's timballo of winter squash and sausages, 158–9
ragù timballo for a picnic in the country, 160–1
veal timballo with an eggplant "shell," 153
Wanda's veal and pork meatballs, 148

basil, 30
spaghetti with raw tomato, garlic, and basil, 22
see also pesto

bavette, 48
bavette with pistachio pesto and shrimp, 48

bean(s):
Alda's pastaciutta with green beans and pecorino, 28
borlotti bean and pasta soup, 124

G

gorgonzola:

festonate with gorgonzola, mascarpone, and walnuts, 59

grappa:

fusilli with porcini mushrooms, aromatic vegetables, and grappa cream sauce, 52

gruyère:

gobbetti with fresh ricotta, gruyère, and nutmeg, 21

H

ham:

capellini timballo with peas, edam, and ham, 156–7

hazelnut(s):

casareccia with Gangivecchio's five-nut pesto, 51

hearty lentil soup with ditalini, 130

herb(s), 10

tagliatelline with zucchini flowers and fresh herbs, 30

see also specific herbs

L

lamb:

baked orecchiette with lamb ragù and melted mozzarella, 136

Paolo's pappardelle with lamb and fava beans braised in red wine, 78

ziti with lamb, lemon, and rosemary, 108

lasagne:

classic baked lasagne, 139–40

fresh cod and zucchini lasagne, 137–8

lasagne ricce with fresh sausages, 93

Paolo's pesto lasagne, 141–2

lasagnette, 46

Giovanna's lasagnette with creamy tomato sauce, toasted almonds, and pecorino cheese, 46

leeks:

Orietta's baked penne casserole with leeks and green peas, 145

lemon:

ziti with lamb, lemon, and rosemary, 108

lentil(s):

hearty lentil soup with ditalini, 130

pasta with lentils ragù, 79

"The Leopard's timballo," 149–50

lettuce:

Mamma's lettuce soup, 127

"straw and hay" with green peas and lettuce in prosciutto cream sauce, 69

linguine, 5

La Cambusa's linguine with shrimp, zucchini, and cherry tomatoes, 60

linguine with scallions, raisins, and turmeric, 38

Orietta's linguine with shrimp and fried artichokes, 92

little penne with potatoes and eggs, 81

lobster:

Mondello-style spaghetti with lobster, 113–14

orecchiette with lobster and prosecco, 104

lumache, 53

lumache rigate with broccoli flowers and turmeric cream, 53

M

maccheroncini, 106

maccheroncini with Marsala, chicken, and prosciutto cotto "for hunters," 106–7

A NOTE ABOUT THE AUTHORS

WANDA TORNABENE and her daughter, GIOVANNA, have run their restaurant out of their thirteenth-century home at Gangivecchio since 1978. Wanda was born in Palermo and, after living in Rome for many years, moved to Gangivecchio in 1948. Giovanna was educated in London but returned to Gangivecchio when she realized it was like living in heaven. Wanda and Giovanna spend most of their time there, and also have a home in Palermo.

CAROLYNN CARREÑO is a freelance writer for magazines and coauthor of cookbooks and divides her time between New York City and Los Angeles. "When Pepe Comes Home for Christmas," a feature she wrote for *Saveur,* was included in the anthology *Best Food Writing 2002.* Another *Saveur* article, "Looking for Guillermo," was nominated for the 2001 James Beard Best Feature Writing award. Her first cookbook, *Once Upon a Tart,* appeared in 2003.

A NOTE ON THE TYPE

The text of this book was set in a typeface named Nofret, designed by Gudrun Zapf–von Hesse in 1986 for Berthold. Von Hesse was born in Frankfurt in 1918. Although primarily a bookbinder, she also designed the typeface Diotima.

Composed by North Market Street Graphics,
Lancaster, Pennsylvania

Printed and bound by Tien Wah Press,
Singapore

Designed by Iris Weinstein